A BRITISH RAILWAYS ILLUSTRATED SPECIAL

A YEAR TO REMEMBER

1957

By
Martin Smith

Springtime in Stockport, 1957. A Manchester-bound local train crossed the 595-yard long viaduct on the evening of 20 May. Urban Stockport nestles below. This magnificent picture gives a superb view of a typical urban environment of the period. PHOTOGRAPH: T.LEWIS

Acknowledgements
Hearty thanks are due to Mr.Bryan Wilson for his advice and assistance during the preparation of this book.
Martin Smith, Coleford, Somerset, August 1999

First published in the United Kingdom in 1999
by Irwell Press
59A, High Street, Clophill,
Bedfordshire MK45 4BE
Printed by The Amadeus Press, Huddersfield

Contents

1957

What a year it was. The world's first space satellite - *Sputnik* - was launched by the former Soviet Union, E.R.N.I.E drew his first Premium Bond numbers, it cost 45 bob to travel from Paddington to Penzance, and Bristol City narrowly avoided relegation to the old Third Division (South). The year of 1957 was also a turning point for Britain's railways - this was particularly so in the case of motive power, as until the latter part of the year steam still reigned virtually supreme on the main lines. Furthermore, in 1957 the railway network itself remained fairly intact, with almost every small town in the land still enjoying a rail service. But that was all about to change. And how!

In railway terms, 1957 marked the beginning of the end of an era - a very, very long era. It was, to a great extent, the last year in which the traditional face of Britain's railway system remained substantially unchanged.

1 June 1957 marked the centenary of the opening of the Crumlin Viaduct, which carried the Pontypool-Aberdare line across the Ebbw Valley. The line across the viaduct closed in 1964 and, although the structure was earmarked for conservation, nobody seemed to inform the authorities – consequently, the viaduct received no maintenance and began to deteriorate rapidly. Nevertheless, in the Summer of 1965 the structure had a bout of cinematic glory when it was used as the location for a chase sequence in the film *Arabesque*, in which those well-known railway enthusiasts, Gregory Peck and Sophia Loren, rode horses across it while Alan Badel tried to exterminate them by shooting from a helicopter. Not long after the viaduct's moment of fame the contractors moved in to commence demolition, but the task defeated five firms of contractors before Messrs.Birds.Birds & Co succeeded in 1967. In our picture, 56XX 0-6-2T No.5647 crosses the viaduct with a Pontypool Road-Neath train. PHOTOGRAPH: JOHN WHITE

What happened was.....

A splendid sight at Liverpool Street in 1957 – the station pilot, J69 No.68619, has just been fully lined out (it was later painted GER blue) while N7 0-6-2T No.69614 sports the new style BR crest. The date is 11 May. PHOTOGRAPH: R.C.RILEY

3.1.57: While undertaking a routine inspection of the main line at Burngullow in Cornwall, a ganger discovered a gaping hole between the up and down tracks. The hole was the shaft of a disused tin mine. During the rest of the day – while safety work was undertaken – through trains terminated at St.Austell or Truro, between which points a shuttle 'bus service was provided.

5.1.57: A3 Pacific No.60106 FLYING FOX shed part of its motion entering Rickmansworth with a Manchester-Marylebone express. The debris short-circuited the electric current, which considerably disrupted Metropolitan Line services.

7.1.57: Regular DMU services commenced between Edinburgh and Glasgow. Two six-coach sets and two three-coach sets were used. These services were in addition to the steam-hauled workings.

7.1.57: At 7.12am, a major accident occurred just to the south of Welwyn Garden City station, when the 7.10pm night express from Aberdeen (train No.113), hauled by A2 4-6-2 No.60520 OWEN TUDOR, was in collision with the 6.18am Baldock-Kings Cross local (train No.1565), hauled by L1 2-6-4T No.67741. The local train had stopped at the up slow platform at Welwyn, and when it departed – 11 minutes late – it was routinely turned on to the up main line to continue, ahead of the Aberdeen express, to its next booked stop at Finsbury Park. In the meantime, the signalman at Welwyn Garden City had accepted the express

from Welwyn North to his up main outer home signal; he intended to hold the express there until the local train had cleared the section, and the signal was, therefore, at danger. The express, however, passed the outer distant signal (which was obviously at caution) without slowing, and it continued past the outer and inner home signals,

A selection of events from the railway year of 1957 – as they happened

despite them being at danger. The express ran forward into the section at 60-65mph and struck the rear of the local train, which was proceeding at about 30-35mph.

The two coaches at the rear of the local train were overturned, and the last coach, a brake second of wooden construction (No.62617 of 1929), was wrecked. The engine of the express train was also overturned and the leading six coaches were derailed; fortunately, though, the coaches remained upright (this was largely thanks to the Buckeye couplings) and sustained little damage. One passenger in the local train was killed and forty-three, mainly from that same train, were injured, five seriously. The driver of the express, although physically unhurt, suffered such severe shock that he had to be detained in hospital. A tragic aftermath was that, later the same night, two gangers

working on the clearance of the line were run down and killed by the breakdown train.

During the obligatory enquiry into the accident, the driver of the express claimed that the outer distant signal which he had passed had been showing a green light. The driver suggested that that signal was notoriously erratic, but the investigating officer, Lt-Col Wilson, found a distinct lack of evidence to support that suggestion. Lt-Col Wilson remarked that, even had the signal been faulty, it did not explain how or why the driver passed the other signals which were against him. The official report blamed the driver of the express for the accident, citing a 'lack of vigilance under weather conditions which required some care' (at the time of the accident, dawn was just breaking and it was generally misty), but the fireman also came in for criticism for 'not providing the assistance in the observation of signals which might have been expected'.

In his remarks and recommendations, Lt-Col Wilson commented that the collision '...was brought about by one of the types of unpredictable human failure for which the safeguard of Automatic Train Control has been designed'. ATC had, of course, first been tried by the GWR as far back as 1906, and by the 1930s had been applied to most GWR main lines. At the time of the Welwyn accident in 1957, however, the nationwide use of ATC had only just been sanctioned.

13.1.57: WR 0-6-0PT No.9401 went on

A surprise visitor to the Eastern Region in 1957 was WR 0-6-0PT No.9401, which went on loan to Stratford shed in February for trials at Bishopsgate and Spitalfields goods depots. The ER would have preferred a 57XX pannier tank – given that the WR was bursting at the seams with panniers at the time, it was, perhaps, surprising that a 57XX couldn't be found. The ER returned No.9401 in June with a polite 'thanks, but no thanks'. Here, No.9401 is seen at Spitalfields on 16 February.
PHOTOGRAPH: R.C.RILEY

loan to Stratford (30A), principally for trials at Bishopsgate goods yard. It was returned to the WR on 11 June.

17.1.57: The first of the Hastings line six-car diesel sets, No.1001, undertook its first main-line tests between Eastleigh and Fareham. Subsequent tests were undertaken as follows:

18 and 20 January: Eastleigh-Andover and Eastleigh-Basingstoke
21 January: Eastleigh-Weymouth
23 January: Eastleigh-Basingstoke
25 January: Eastleigh-Southampton Terminus-Alton-Eastleigh-Andover Junction-Eastleigh
29 January: Eastleigh-Southampton Central-Eastleigh
30 January: Eastleigh-Southampton Central-Portsmouth-Southampton Central-Eastleigh.

The unit gave general satisfaction – apart from minor problems with the fuel pump on 29 January – and was reported to have notched up 75mph on at least one occasion. It departed from Eastleigh on 6 February, bound for Ashford, thence to its designated duties on the Hastings line.

20.1.57: Diesel locomotives Nos.10201 and 10202, built in 1951 to a design which had originated with the Southern Railway, made their debut in Scotland, working to Glasgow with the 10.00am from Euston. They were subsequently used in conjunction with ex-LMS diesels 10000 and 10001 on the Royal Scot; the usual practice was for 10201 and 10202 to work the up Royal Scot and return north with the 9.10pm Euston-Glasgow sleeper.

23.1.57: The main Edinburgh-Glasgow line was blocked for about 12 hours due to a landslide near Falkirk High station.

28.1.57: The title of the Royal Duchy was bestowed on the 1.30pm Paddington-Penzance and the 11.00am Penzance-Paddington. The inaugural down train was hauled as far as Plymouth by No.6000 KING GEORGE V, which sported a new style headboard incorporating the Cornish coat of arms. Although No.6000 did the honours on the first day, in normal service the duty was usually handled by Castles.

2.57: Early in the month, the turntable at Carlisle (Kingmoor) shed was under repair, which meant that engines had to use the Bog Junction triangle for turning. During the repairs to the 'table, Kingmoor's last Westinghouse-fitted engine, ex-Caledonian 0-6-0 No.56235, was used to supply compressed air for the riveting work.

2.2.57: The leading diesel engine on the down 'Royal Scot', No.10001, caught fire when approaching Roade. It was taken off the train, and No.10000 hauled the train solo to Rugby where two 5MTs took over.

7.2.57: WR 0-6-0PT No.1646 started its journey from Croes Newydd to Helmsdale, to replace the last Highland Railway 0-4-4T on branch duties between The Mound and Dornoch.

9.2.57: An accident involving three trains occurred at Chapel-en-le-Frith (South) station. Two people died, but it could have been far worse. The accident was caused by the failure of the braking system on 8F 2-8-0 No.48188 – the fracturing of a joint in the pipe leading to the driver's steam brake valve meant that the locomotive's brakes became non-operational. No.48188 had not long left Buxton with the 11.05am freight to Arpley (Warrington) when the incident occurred. The fracturing of the steam pipe filled the cab with scalding steam, but the driver and firemen, after repeated efforts, managed to get the regulator partly closed and to apply the hand brake on the tender. However, the train was being banked at the rear, and the crew of the banking engine were completely unaware of the trouble on the footplate of No.48188, and so, while the driver and fireman of No.48188 were desperately trying to stop the train, the banker kept pushing. Despite the valiant efforts of No.48188's crew, the engine and train cleared the summit and started the descent, effectively out of control, down the long incline towards Chapel-en-le-Frith.

The driver ordered the fireman to jump down from the footplate and try

In the early hours of 5 April 1957, a fire caused extensive damage to Cannon Street station signal box. Inevitably, this brought about a major disruption – how else could one account for Cannon Street being *this* quiet on a Friday morning?
PHOTOGRAPHS: R.C.RILEY

You'll Remember those Black and White Days...

In May 1957 new colour light signalling came into full operation at Dumfries. OK – you can't actually *see* the signalling here, but it's the excuse we require for including this excellent picture of Jubilee No.45732 SANSPAREIL heading north through Dumfries on 29 June 1957. PHOTOGRAPH: BRIAN MORRISON

to pin down some of the wagon brakes, but although he succeeded in pinning down the brakes of six or seven wagons, it would have needed sixteen wagon brakes to be applied before the train could be brought under control. This was simply impossible. Despite the fireman's brave effort, the train – 33 loaded wagons and a brake van, some 650 tons, plus 125 tons of engine and tender – inevitably gathered speed down the incline. This was no gentle descent – it varied between 1 in 58 and 1 in 70 for seven miles to Whaley Bridge, with just two easements to 1 in 150 through Dove Holes and Chapel-en-le-Frith stations. Near the start of the descent the train passed Dove Holes signal box, and the signalman, on seeing the manner of the train's approach, realised something was desperately amiss and knew that he had to make a split second decision between two courses of action. If he diverted the runaway train into the loop it was likely that the train would run through the trap siding and then into the end of the Doves Holes platform wall, with potentially disastrous results. Alternatively, he could allow the train to continue on the main line in the hope that the driver could regain control, but the danger in this instance was that a Rowsley-Stockport freight train (also hauled by an 8F) was still in section. The signalman opted for the latter course of action, as he considered that the Rowsley-Stockport train should be sufficiently far in front for a collision to be avoided. That train was, in fact, still making its way slowly towards Chapel-en-le-Frith.

The Dove Holes signalman, on realising the danger and giving the runaway train the main line, promptly telephoned ahead to Chapel-en-le-Frith to inform them of events. At this time, the 10.20am Manchester-Buxton passenger train – a two-car DMU – had just pulled into the up (southbound) platform at Chapel-en-le-Frith station but, fortunately, the station staff, having been made aware of the scenario, were able to evacuate the train. By now, the Rowsley-Stockport freight train was entering Chapel-en-le-Frith station, and its crew were, until then, totally unaware that there was a runaway train behind them. At the station, railway staff on the platform waved and shouted to the crew of the Rowsley-Stockport train to accelerate away, but a sudden sprint was impossible as the train weighed some 750 tons and, furthermore, several wagons had their brakes pinned down. At about this time the runaway train had emerged from Eaves Tunnel, less than a mile from Chapel-en-le-Frith station, and was heading at speed down the gradient towards the station.

One can only imagine the atmosphere at Chapel-en-le-Frith station as the railway staff watched, with total helplessness, the approach of the runaway train on the down line. The diesel train in the up platform had, fortunately, been evacuated with commendable efficiency, but ahead of the runaway train on the down line was the Rowsley-Stockport train, which had no means of escape whatsoever. The runaway train was doing an estimated 55mph when it

ploughed into the rear of the Rowsley-Stockport train. The brake van and the three rear wagons of the Rowsley train were destroyed, and the shock wave through the train was such that four wagons near the front of the train (some 200yds ahead of the point of impact) were derailed. The runaway engine fell on its right hand side against the up platform wall, its tender striking and demolishing the signal box. The leading thirty wagons were piled on top of the rear vehicles of the Rowsley train and formed a mass of debris 25ft high. Of the three remaining wagons in the train, two were derailed and one, plus the brake van, remained undamaged and still on the rails. The leading coach of the DMU which was standing at Chapel-en-le-Frith was struck by the runaway engine.

Driver Axon, who had been on the footplate of the runaway train, and the guard of the Rowsley freight train were killed. It was appreciated that, had it not been for the bravery of Driver Axon, the accident could have been far worse – had he abandoned the engine the train could have continued to Whaley Bridge, by which time, it was calculated, it would have been doing almost 80mph. That was, of course, if it hadn't already been thrown off the rails on one of the many curves – with potentially catastrophic consequences. Also, by remaining on the footplate, amid scalding steam escaping from the fractured brake pipe, Driver Axon had been able to warn the Dove Holes signalman. Driver Axon was posthumously awarded the George Cross for outstanding devotion to duty.

On Monday 6 May 1957 the inaugural diesel service to Hastings – the 5.18pm ex-Cannon Street – starts on its journey.
PHOTOGRAPH: BRIAN MORRISON

Probably the luckiest escapee was the Chapel-en-le-Frith signalman – the 'box was completely demolished by the tender of the runaway engine, but the signalman was somehow thrown clear and came out relatively unscathed.

The official investigation into the accident homed in on the fractured steam pipe. The ensuing report explained that pipe, which was 1.125in in diameter and made of brass, had a butt joint at its lower end where it was connected to the brake valve casting. The joint was made by inserting 'walkerite' (a packing material made of impregnated asbestos) between a collar brazed on the end of the pipe and the screwed end of the brake valve casting, a union nut then being screwed up until the joint was steam-tight. It was this joint which had failed on No.48188.

It was an accepted fact of life that these joints would work loose, primarily due to the vibration on the footplate, but the leaks were usually stopped by tightening the nut or, if necessary, by repacking. In the case of No.48188, however, the brake steam pipe seemed to have been a regular source of trouble. It was reported that in April 1955 the engine had had a 'heavy intermediate' at Horwich, during which the steam pipe would have been routinely annealed. Since then, the engine had run 38,200 miles. The engine's repair card, kept at its home shed at Warrington, revealed that between November 1955 and February 1957 there had been no less than ten reports of 'brake steam pipe nut blowing' (far more than was usual with 8Fs), but each time the blowing was cured simply by tightening the union nut. It was not realised that the

brazing inside the union nut was gradually disintegrating, and it was this which finally failed with such awful consequences. The condition of the brazing and the internal joints was revealed only by a metallurgical examination after the accident, and the inspecting officer emphasised that the fitters at Warrington shed were in no way to blame – '...the reports (of blowing) were not sufficiently unusual to attract special attention and hence the deterioration of the joint remained unnoticed'.

The official report into the accident stressed that nobody was to blame. It was, quite simply, 'an accident'. The report noted, with satisfaction, that the LMR had subsequently instigated a programme whereby the butted joints on brake steam pipes would be routinely replaced by coned joints. This programme would, of course, take several years to complete, and in the meantime it was intended to take down and examine all butted joints at regular intervals. Furthermore, an improved method of brazing had been adopted. The report concluded with the suggestion that the collision might not have occurred if continuous vacuum brakes had been in operation throughout the train, although it was acknowledged that BR had recently announced their intention to equip all freight rolling stock with continuous brakes in due course.

17.2.57: T9 4-4-0 No.30319 and M7 0-4-4T No.30026 were involved in the filming of 'The Railway Children' at Baynards, on the Horsham-Guildford line.

23.2.57: Football specials were commonplace throughout the 1950s,

but it should not go unremarked that for a fourth round tie of the Amateur Cup between Wycombe Wanderers and Ilford, three ten-coach specials were laid on. How things have changed. These days, the entire crowd at some league matches wouldn't fill three trains.

27.2.57: In the early hours, there was a break-away on the 12.35am Ferme Park-New England empties while the train was in Potters Bar Tunnel. The wagons ran back to collide with the 2.15am Kings Cross-Grantham newspapers. Nobody was injured, but later that morning the rush hour traffic into Kings Cross was severely disrupted.

4.3.57: The former LMR Leeds (City) and Wakefield Operating Districts were transferred to the NER.

9.3.57: Robert Whitelegg died at the age of 85. He was best known as the designer of the first Baltic (4-6-4) tanks to work on a British railway – these were built in 1912 for the London Tilbury & Southend. In 1922 he brought out another class of 4-6-4Ts for his then-current employers, the Glasgow & South Western.

19.3.57: Although the new-style BR crest had been displayed in June 1956, it took a little while for it to be applied. As far as can be determined it was first used at Caerphilly Works in March 1957, 0-6-2T No.5680 becoming the trend-setter on the 19th of the month.

20.3.57: Standard Class 4 2-6-4T No.80154 became the 1,211th and final locomotive to be constructed at Brighton Works. It was allocated from new to Brighton shed (75A), and spent the rest of its working life – a mere ten years – on the Southern Region.

31.3.57: Train services into and out of

St.Pancras were completely suspended from 4.40am and 8.00am while a 76ft-wide signal gantry was erected across the tracks at the north end of the station.

3.57: During the month, the original 1848 roof at Lincoln Central station was completely replaced.

5.4.57: During the early hours of the morning, a fire broke out in the relay room of Cannon Street station signal box. The 'box – a wooden structure dating to 1926 – was severely damaged and all signalling and tele-communications were put out of action. Following the fire, the electric power at the station and its approaches was necessarily cut off.

This meant that the suburban electric services to and from Cannon Street had to be suspended; these services accounted for the vast majority of the 200-plus services into and out of the station each weekday. The only services which could operate were steam-hauled, and these had to be hand signalled into Platforms 1 and 2. For the start of the following week – Monday 8 April – an emergency timetable was introduced. That timetable was revised for the subsequent week, and by this time Cannon Street - which had had its power restored and was equipped with a temporary frame – was able to handle some 160 trains each day.

9.4.57: 2-6-2T No.40139 fell into the turntable pit at Ilkley. The engine was pulled out by Class 5 No.73150.

13/14.4.57: The new signal box at Weymouth was brought into use. It had 116 levers, and replaced the old Station and Junction 'boxes (each of which had 44-levers) and two ground frames.

15.4.57: A collision occurred at Portsmouth & Southsea. The empty stock to form the 5.45pm Portsmouth-Cardiff collided with the 4.45pm Portsmouth-Cardiff which was leaving the station. Four passengers were injured. The breakdown crane was summoned from Eastleigh, but one of its bogies developed a fault *en route* and it damaged the down line between Green Lanes and Fratton. The line was reopened throughout at 10.00am the following day.

24.4.57: An A4 Pacific worked out of Paddington for the first time since the locomotive exchanges of 1948. This instance involved No.60029 WOODCOCK, which worked a 12-coach special taking members of the Ian Allan Locospotters Club to Doncaster Works.

29.4.57: The engine shed at Seaton (Rutland) was virtually destroyed by a fire which spread from the embankment of the Midland main line. Although a sub-shed of Rugby (2A) for many years, between 1955 and 1958 Seaton looked to Market Harborough to supply its locomotives – these were used principally on the Uppingham branch. At the time of the fire, the shed, which was a single-road timber built structure, was empty. Seaton remained operational as a stabling point until the cessation of the Uppingham branch goods services in 1961; since the fire, its locomotives – usually Ivatt or Standard 2-6-2Ts – had been stabled in the open.

29.4.57: It was not a good day for fires... Ex-GWR diesel railcar No.29 (working in conjunction with No.24) burst into flames near Reading while working the 7.45am Slough to Reading. The local fire brigade had to be summoned. The railcar was, however, subsequently repaired, and continued in service until 1962. In Spring 1957, incidentally, thirty ex-GWR railcars were still operational; they were distributed among Southall, Reading, Bristol, Leamington, Stourbridge, Worcester, Cheltenham and Ebbw Junction.

4.5.57: A wedding special worked from Liverpool Street to Framlingham. It was hauled by B12/3 4-6-0 No.61571 and comprised five first class bogies and a buffet car. It was believed to be the first (and last??) time a B12 had traversed the Framlingham branch.

4.57: During the month, the last ex-LNWR 'Cauliflower' 0-6-0, No.58427, which had been withdrawn from service in 1955, was finally cut up at Crewe.

6.5.57: The new colour light signalling system at Dumfries came into full operation. Two new signalboxes - Dumfries Station and Dumfries South - replaced four older manual 'boxes.

10.5.57: WR 0-6-0PT No.2069 took up temporary duties as the Carriage Works shunter at Wolverton.

5.57: A new 70-lever signal box was brought into use at Denbigh. It replaced three older 'boxes – Denbigh Nos.1 and 2, and Mold & Denbigh Junction.

5.57: The first application of the new 'D' prefix was seen on a diesel locomotive. The locomotive concerned was diesel shunter No.D3455, which was completed at Darlington Works early in May. As far as can be determined, the first existing diesels to be renumbered in accordance with the new scheme were Nos.13004 and 13036 (D3004 and D3036), which were dealt with during a visit to Swindon Works in November 1957.

6.67: The new-style BR crest filtered through to the Scottish locomotive works, being used for the first time at

Banbury was the scene of much remodelling and rebuilding in 1957. On 25 April, while the down side of the station was in the course of rebuilding, Austerity 2-8-0 No.90563 passes through with a mineral train. **PHOTOGRAPH: R.C.RILEY**

On 9 July 1957, LM Pacific No.46256 SIR WILLIAM A. STANIER F.R.S. ascends Shap with a Euston-Carlisle express.
PHOTOGRAPH: LES ELSEY

Cowlairs early in June 1957.

1.6.57: Centenary of the opening of Crumlin Viaduct across the Ebbw Valley. The spectacular structure was 553yds in length and had a maximum height of 200ft. It originally incorporated 2,390 tons of iron.

3.6.57: New relief line and platform at Banbury brought into use.

3.6.57: The very first of the 'new breed' of main-line diesel locomotives, D8000, was formally handed over to the BTC by the makers, the English Electric Co.

5.6.57: Fatal accident at Hayburn Wyke occupation crossing, between Scarborough and Whitby. A train was in collision with a road vehicle, the driver of which was killed.

7.6.57: 8F 2-8-0 No.48188 became the first locomotive to receive the new style BR crest at Derby Works. The locomotive had been in for repairs after its accident at Chapel-en-le-Frith. Also at about this time, Derby started using the 'D' prefix for its new diesel locomotives; the first to carry the prefix from new was D3358 which was destined for the Western Region.

11.6.57: Standard Class 2 2-6-2T No.84029 became the 2,269th and last steam locomotive to be completed at Darlington Works. The locomotive was allocated from new to Ramsgate (74B), and this was in itself another 'last' – it was the very last new steam locomotive to be delivered to the Southern Region.

13.6.57: Brand-new Standard Class 5 4-6-0 No.73154 (one of the Caprotti versions) was steamed at Derby Works to claim the unwanted distinction of being the last of 2,995 steam locomotives to be constructed there in 106 years. No.73154 was allocated from new to St.Rollox (65B).

15.6.57: During the four-week period ending 15 June, WR 0-6-0PT No.5423 (82D) became the first 'matchbox' to wear a lined green livery. This had been applied at Caerphilly Works while the engine was in for a 'heavy'.

16.6.57: New 24-lever signalbox brought into use at Honiton.

16.6.57: Dorchester engine shed (71C) closed and its ten daily turns were transferred to the WR shed at Weymouth (82F), where additional facilities had been provided. Despite its ten daily turns and a staff of thirty-three, Dorchester had actually had no allocation of its own since March 1955. Following closure, short work was made of the shed, a report in October noting that: '...little remained apart from two roads, the hoist, a heap of timber and brick debris'.

17.6.57: The start of the summer timetable saw the introduction of no less than five named trains. Probably the best-known of these was The Caledonian. The train, described as a 'limited load flyer', was aimed principally at the business market – even in 1957, airlines had started to

The Caledonian made its debut on Monday 17 June 1957, being scheduled to run from Euston to Glasgow Central in 6 hours 40 minutes. The following year – on 4 July – No.46241 CITY OF EDINBURGH waits to depart from Euston. PHOTOGRAPH: T.J.EDGINGTON

You'll Remember those Black and White Days...

capture some of the Anglo-Scottish business traffic, and it was hoped that the new train would regain some of this traffic for the railways. The Caledonian comprised eight coaches (there were two sets) which could accommodate 84 first- and 120 second-class passengers, and was timed to complete the 401 miles between Euston and Glasgow Central in 6hrs 40 mins – i.e. just within the magic 'mile a minute' schedule for the entire journey. The LMR had, in fact, been deliberating about a high speed London-Glasgow service for some time, but it had been considered that proposed schedules would create considerable operating difficulties. It wasn't until early 1957 that the problems were circumvented.

The first day's up Caledonian was hauled by No.46229 DUCHESS OF HAMILTON, which left Glasgow Central at 8.30am and arrived at Euston at 3.10pm. The down working left Euston at 4.15pm behind No.46242 CITY OF GLASGOW, but although it was scheduled to arrive in Glasgow at 10.55pm its time-keeping was unavoidably affected by the aftermath of the derailment, earlier that day, of the down 'Mid-day Scot' at Uddingston Junction. Later in 1957, The Caledonian notched up some very impressive performances. On 7 August No.46229 DUCHESS OF HAMILTON completed the up journey in 6hrs 27mins, which included – under a special schedule which was in force for one day only – an average of 74.1mph start-to-stop for the 158 miles from Crewe to Euston. A special schedule was also in force on 5 September when No.46244 KING GEORGE VI did the up journey in an impressive 6hrs 3mins.

Another business-orientated move which manifested itself at the start of the 1957 summer timetable on 17 June was a revision of the working of The Talisman. This train had been inaugurated in September 1956 to provide a fast service between Kings Cross and Edinburgh via the East Coast Main Line, but for the 1957 summer timetable the train was separated into the Morning Talisman and Afternoon Talisman. The same two sets of stock were used day in, day out on 'Talisman' duties – 786 miles for each set each day – and so all the coaches concerned were fitted with Timken roller bearings.

Also for the start of the 1957 summer timetable, the 9.15am St.Pancras-Edinburgh and the 10.05am Edinburgh-St.Pancras assumed the title of The Waverley. In pre-war times, those workings had operated as The Thames-Forth. Also taking effect on the same day, the name of The Royal Highlander was revived for the 7.20pm Euston-Inverness and the 5.15pm Inverness-Euston sleepers. On the Western Region, as from 17

June the title of The Mayflower was applied to the existing 8.30am Plymouth-Padington and 5.30pm Paddington-Plymouth. On the train's very first day of operation the timetables were disrupted because of three special boat trains which had to be run from Plymouth, but it was deemed inadvisable to delay the inaugural up Mayflower as HRH Princess Margaret was on board. The train was therefore run in two portions - the first portion was headed by No.6028 KING GEORGE VI and, calling only at Newton Abbot and Taunton, it arrived at Paddington on time at 1.25pm. The second portion – which made the stops omitted by the first part – did not reach Paddington until 2.00pm. On the following day, The Mayflower encountered problems of a different sort. No.6007 KING WILLIAM III failed at Taunton with the up train, and 40 minutes were lost waiting for the replacement engine, which took the form of No.4924 EYDON HALL. The Hall struggled with the 15-coach loading, losing another 20 minutes between Taunton and Westbury, and so No.5999 WOLLATON HALL was attached as a pilot at Westbury. The train arrived at Paddington one hour late.

17.6.57: BR proudly announced that the new summer timetable included 98 runs which were timed at 60mph or more; of these, 41 were on the LMR, 31 on the WR, 25 on the E and NER, and one on the SR. But it wasn't all good news, especially for those who required 'on-train' catering. It was announced that instead of a three-course lunch costing 7/6d, the only option would be a four-course lunch costing 9/6d; afternoon tea was to go up from 2/6d to 3/-, while a cup of coffee would cost 9d instead of 8d. A contemporary account of a lunch on The Flying Scotsman noted that, instead of the customary fish course, diners were offered '...a watery mess of ungarnished scrambled egg followed by that faithful standby, tinned fruit salad and a slab of ice cream...'. To redress the balance, that same account was highly complimentary of the standard of catering on The Caledonian. As for fares, for the summer timetable the London Midland Region introduced a new rail rover ticket which, for just £9, gave freedom to travel on any of the region's trains. That was stunningly good value – in 1957, two return trips between London and Carlisle would have cost £9.8s.0d. Another bonus – this time on the whole of BR – was that for the duration of the summer timetable there was a reduction of 4/- in the £ on charges for dogs, bicycles and perambulators which accompanied passengers.

17.6.57: The down 'Mid-day Scot' was passing over points on the down main line at Uddington Junction (between

Motherwell and Glasgow) when the 5th, 8th, 10th, 11th and 12th coaches were derailed and struck some wagons which were standing in the down siding. One passenger was killed and three (including the guard) required hospitalisation.

17.6.57: Stage One of the Hastings diesel scheme came into full operation.

17.6.57: Brand new 'Type 1' diesel-electric D8000 ran from the Vulcan Foundry to Edge Hill depot, and later worked to Penrith and back with a test train. This was one of the regular trial diagrams for Vulcan-built engines.

18.6.57: Former LB&SC Atlantic No.32424 BEACHY HEAD – a locomotive with a very enthusiastic fan club – blew out its left-hand front end, badly damaging the connecting rod. It was feared that this would lead to the withdrawal of the engine – the last survivor of its class – but it was repaired, using some parts from withdrawn classmate No.32425. It was, however, 23 July before No.32424 was steamed again.

23.6.57: Sunday services were introduced on the Deeside branch (Aberdeen-Ballater) in an attempt to increase the overall usage of the line. Initially, six trains each way were planned for the Sunday services. At this time the branch was worked mainly by Standard 2-6-4Ts, and the previous month Nos.80111, 80112, 80114 and 80115 had been transferred from Polmadie to Kittybrewster in exchange for Nos.80106-80109 – the reason for the exchange was that the outgoing engines did not have a recess for the tablet exchanging apparatus, whereas the incoming engines were suitably equipped.

28.6.57 to 30.6.57: The 'Modern Railway Travel' exhibition was staged at Battersea Wharf in London. The principal purpose of the exhibition was to display some features of the modernisation plan; among the exhibits were DELTIC, D8000, diesel-electric shunter No.13354, multiple-unit stock and ordinary modern rolling stock.

6.57: The withdrawal of D16/3 4-4-0 No.62546 CLAUD HAMILTON from Yarmouth (South Town) shed during the month of June was not as major an event as it might have seemed. To most enthusiasts, the 'correct' wearer of that name was regarded as LNER No.2500, and it was only when that loco had been withdrawn in May 1947 that the nameplates had been transferred to No.2546 (BR No.62546).

1.7.57: K1 2-6-0 No.62029, hauling a 35-wagon coal train, ran into the rear of a four-car DMU set at Hexham station. Most fortunately, the DMU's passengers had just disembarked.

1.7.57: The engine shed at Watlington (a sub to Didcot, 81E) closed – this was a consequence of the withdrawal of passenger services on the Princes Risborough-Watlington branch.

16.7.57: Britannia No.70045 was named LORD ROWALLAN at Euston. Lord Rowallan was the Chief Scout, and the naming of the locomotive coincided with the World Scout Jamboree which was held that year at Sutton Park, Sutton Coldfield. The Jamboree actually ran from 1 to 12 August, but there were a number of incoming special trains prior to formal opening. In all, during July and August an estimated 190 excursion and special trains were run in connection with the Jamboree.

22.7.57: The former Stratford & Midland Junction engine shed at Stratford-upon-Avon finally closed. The shed had lost its own allocation of engines in 1953 when it had been transferred to the WR, but despite the regional switch Saltley (its erstwhile LMR parent depot) continued to provide it with locomotives – sometimes as many as six at a time, usually 0-6-0s, principally for use via the SMJ line to Northampton or Bedford. Following the shed's closure, visiting LM locos – usually a couple of 4Fs from Bedford and a couple from Northampton – were stabled outside the local WR shed.

5.8.57: A bridge spanning a stream about three miles north of Rhayader (on the Builth Wells-Moat Lane section) collapsed; this happened 30 minutes after the passage of the 7.45am passenger train from Builth Wells. A temporary bridge was operational by the following morning.

9.8.57: Accident near Staines Central – 700 class 0-6-0 No.30688, running light engine, overturned after colliding

with a Windsor-Waterloo electric train.

27.8.57: Class 5 No.45370 derailed near Rugby No.7 Signal Box at about 8.15pm. The engine was running light to Coventry to work the 10.00pm Coventry-Curzon Street goods. It was rerailed the following morning.

31.8.57: The first of the year's hop pickers trains arrived at Bodiam on the Kent & East Sussex line. The trains had worked through from London Bridge, albeit with the obligatory engine change at Robertsbridge.

8.57: The new BR crest was applied for the first time at Inverurie Works. As far as can be determined, the first locomotives to have the new crest applied at Inverurie were ex-Caley 4-4-0 No.54495, ex-North British (J37) 0-6-0 No.64553 and Caley 'Jumbo' 0-6-0 No.57249.

16.8.57: New diesel locomotive D8000 arrived at Toton for a series of tests from 19th to 31st of the month.

9.9.57: For the last week of public passenger services on the SR's Bentley-Bordon branch, M7 No.30110 (70C) and 'Ironclad' motor set 384 were used.

14.9.57: Builth Wells shed, a sub of Brecon (89B), closed, and its duties were transferred to the ex-LNWR shed at Builth Road. Prior to 1955 Builth Wells had usually accommodated an 0-4-2T – since 1937 this had often been No.5801 – but latterly the shed had had no permanent allocation, a pair of LM-type 2-6-0s being sent along from Brecon for a fortnight at a time.

16.9.57: For the start of the winter timetable, the Western Region introduced The Cathedrals Express, which took in the 7.45am Hereford-

Paddington and 4.45pm return; both workings were usually rostered for a Castle throughout, but on 30 September the WR's most famous locomotive, No.6000 KING GEORGE V, was given charge of the Paddington-Swindon leg.

The 'Cathedrals' was yet another addition to the WR's list of trains which were formed of chocolate and cream stock. By the autumn of 1957 the list comprised fourteen trains: The Cornish Riviera Express, Torbay Express, The Royal Duchy, The Bristolian, The Merchant Venturer, The Red Dragon, The Pembroke Coast Express, Capitals United Express, The Inter City, Cambrian Coast Express, The Cornishman, Cheltenham Spa Express, The Cathedrals Express and The Mayflower. Earlier in 1957, there had been criticism of the sloppy manner in which the Red Dragon and Inter City had been formed; despite the official edict of chocolate and cream, at that time the sets had included GW dining cars which were still in red and cream.

Also on 16 September, yet another named train appeared on the East Coast Main Line. This was The Fair Maid, which was based on the existing 7.45am Kings Cross-Edinburgh and 7.30am Edinburgh-Kings Cross. For the new service, those trains were retimed to leave at 7.50am and 8.30am respectively and were extended to and from Perth. The inaugural up train (on 16 September) left Edinburgh behind A4 No.60027 MERLIN, which was replaced at Newcastle by A1 No.60156 GREAT CENTRAL for the rest of the trip to Kings Cross. The first down train was taken out of Kings Cross by A4 No.60015 QUICKSILVER; it was relieved at Newcastle by No.60027, which worked home to Edinburgh. A Perth South 5MT took over at Edinburgh for the final leg. The sets used for The Fair Maid each comprised nine coaches (309 tons tare), all painted maroon and wearing the new BR crests.

Two other named trains made their debut with the new winter timetable – both were revivals of pre-war names. One was The Lancastrian, the title being bestowed on 16 September on an established Euston-Manchester return working; the down train was the 7.55am (SX) or 8.45am (SO) ex-Euston, and the return was the 4.00pm from Manchester. The other was The Palatine which, from 16 September, was applied to the 7.55am St.Pancras-Manchester Central and the 2.25pm return.

16.9.57: The first stage of the Hampshire diesel scheme came into operation – this took in services between Salisbury and Portsmouth via Southampton. Hitherto, the services between Southampton and Portsmouth had been frequently criticised for being among the slowest

The winter timetable of 1957 saw the debut of four named trains. One was The Fair Maid, which was based on existing services between Kings Cross and Edinburgh; A1 Pacific No.60121 SILURIAN approaches Finsbury Park with the down train. PHOTOGRAPH: BRIAN MORRISON

You'll Remember those Black and White Days...

Among the five named trains to be introduced with the Summer timetable for 1957 was The Afternoon Talisman, which operated between Kings Cross and Edinburgh. Despite any means of formal identification, we can assure you that this *is* the Afternoon Talisman – it is the northbound train, approaching Selby in the charge of A4 Pacific No.60025 FALCON. PHOTOGRAPH: BRIAN MORRISON

on the Southern Region, while services between Southampton and Salisbury had been considered even worse. On the day before the commencement of the diesel services, the last two steam-worked stopping trains from Portsmouth & Southsea to Southampton had been the 9.03pm (hauled by No.76027) and the 10.26pm (hauled by No.76015). The new diesel services weren't the instantaneous, wholesale success which had been envisaged. During the first few months there were frequent failures, many of which were attributed to overloading - the crews were usually blamed for letting this happen.

16.9.57: The former NBR shed at Stirling Shore Road (sub of 63B) closed. Its dozen or so locomotives – all ex-NB and LNE types – were transferred to Stirling South or, as a contemporary report had it '...were crammed into indifferent accommodation at Stirling South'.

22.9.57: As part of the modernisation scheme at Newcastle-upon-Tyne, colour light signalling came into operation at the west end of Newcastle Central.

23.9.57: Cheltenham-Honeybourne line closed for engineering work. It did not reopen until 15 December.

30.9.57: 9F 2-10-0 No.92178 – the first of the class to be built with a double chimney – was completed at Swindon. The engine was designated for the Eastern Region.

9.57: The new-style BR crest finally reached St.Rollox Works. Among the first locomotives to have it applied there were Nos.45473, 55260, 57559, 73100 and 80001.

9.57: Standard 9F 2-10-0 No.92178 was the first of the class to be built with a double chimney. After emerging from Swindon Works it underwent various steaming trials on the stationary plant and was subjected to road tests between Reading and Stoke Gifford before being despatched to its permanent home at New England. The double chimney arrangement was considered a worthwhile addition and so, starting from No.92183 – which was completed at Swindon in December 1957 – all other 9Fs (except Giesl-fitted No.92250) were turned out with double chimneys. Nine other 9Fs which had been built with single chimneys were later fitted with double chimneys. Overall, though, it was eventually conceded that double chimneys provided negligible benefits when the locomotives were employed on their customary freight duties.

9.57: BR took into stock three 8F 2-8-0s which it had purchased from the Ministry of Supply. The three had been built by the North British Locomotive Co to the standard Stanier design in 1940/41 and had been among the 259 representatives of the type to be taken into WD stock (our three had, in fact, seen service on the Iranian State Railways in 1941-44). They – and two others – returned to the Longmoor Military Railway in 1954/55, but whereas the other pair were transferred to the Military Port at Cairnryan in Scotland, our trio were retained at Longmoor until 1957, when they were sold to BR. Apparently, BR seemed to be under the impression that they were Austerity-type 2-8-0s and therefore allotted them

Nos.90733-90735, but when the error of identity was realised they were allotted, instead, Nos.48773-48775. Happily, No.48773 is still with us, having been saved for preservation after its withdrawal by BR in the 1960s.

16.10.57: Standard Class 4 2-6-0 No.76114 emerged from Doncaster Works, thus becoming the very last of 2,228 steam locomotives to be completed there. It was allocated from new to St.Rollox (65B).

19.10.57: The platforms were removed from Highgate Road station. The station had, in fact, been closed to passengers since 1 March 1918!

23.10.57: BTH 'Type 1' diesel-electric D8200 made a trial run with one coach from the Yorkshire Engine Co at Meadowhall to Chinley and return.

28.10.57: Kentish Town-Barking services were truncated at East Ham so that work on the new bridge spanning the main lines at Barking – the Barking Flyover – could commence in earnest.

31.10.57: Brush Traction Ltd 'Type 2' 1250hp diesel-electric D5500 was officially handed over to the Eastern Region at a ceremony at the maker's Loughborough works. During October, the locomotive had undergone trials between Loughborough and Manchester, and had been reported to have coped satisfactorily with a 13-coach load of 393 tons on the steeply graded Peak Forest section between Derby and Chinley. D5500 had been completed five weeks ahead of schedule.

10.57: The SR's oldest locomotive, LBSC 'Terrier' No.32636, was overhauled and repainted at Brighton Works. It had been built in September 1872.

2.11.57: A surprising 'first' – the first BR Pacific to appear at Newcastle was No.72002 CLAN CAMPBELL, which worked in with a goods from Edinburgh.

4.11.57: Newport (IOW) shed (70G) closed, and its remaining duties were transferred to Ryde (70H). At the time of its closure, Newport had already lost its permanent allocation of locomotives although a couple of O2s were stored there.

4.11.57: The Hampshire diesel scheme came into full operation with the introduction of diesel services on the Southampton-Alton and Portsmouth-Eastleigh-Andover routes. Additional diesel services between Portsmouth and Southampton were also provided. On the Alton route, the diesels displaced the push-pull trains which had been the haunt of M7 0-4-4Ts. Perversely, though, on the Andover route, in May 1958 some of the diesel services were diagrammed to terminate at Eastleigh and so push-pull workings (with M7s) were provided between there and Andover.

5.11.57: At Kilsby, just to the south of

Rugby, an articulated lorry plunged over a bridge and came to rest on the main line. The down 'Lancastrian', hauled by Class 5 No.45595, struck some of the debris, parts of which were carried into Kilsby tunnel before the train could be brought to a halt. It could have been much much worse... After much hard work the lines were reopened at 3.00 the following morning, but just five hours later the lines were blocked again. This time, the culprit was a pick-up goods train, of which the brake van and a wagon left the rails during shunting manouevres at Welton station, at the south end of Kilsby tunnel. The line was reopened – for the second time – later that afternoon.

15.11.57: Epping shed (sub to Stratford, 30A) was closed following the electrification of the Epping-Ongar section. (*See separate feature*)

17.11.57: New B.T.H. diesel-electric D8200 arrived at Willesden shed, and was formally handed over to the BTC on the following day. It was subsequently dispatched to Devons Road shed.

25.11.57: North British-built diesel-hydraulic D600 – bound eventually for the Western Region – made its public debut, working a three-coach special from South Side Carriage Sidings (Glasgow) to Kilmarnock and return.

29.11.57: Horwich Works completed its 1,840[th] and last steam locomotive. This was Class 4 No.76099, which was allocated from new to Corkerhill (67A).

11.57: The improvements at Abergavenny (Monmouth Road) station were in their final stages. The work included an extension of the up platform to about twice its former length; this dispensed with the need for trains to pull up on a rising gradient.

11.57: Crewe Works completed the construction of its first diesel shunters, D3419-D3421, which were designated for the Western Region. Swindon, meanwhile, was constructing 204hp diesel shunters and 9Fs for the Eastern Region and Class 4 4-6-0s for the LM Region. And then there were the 350hp diesel shunters for the Southern Region which were built at Darlington...

4.12.57: The worst accident in the history of the Southern Railway and its predecessors – and the third worst in British railway history – occurred near St.Johns station, Lewisham, on Wednesday 4 December 1957. The ensuing Ministry of Transport report – normally an unemotional, somewhat aloof document – recognised it as a 'disaster'.

On the day in question a dense fog enveloped much of London, and the evening rush hour trains were running very late. So late, in fact, that the scheduled 4.56pm Cannon Street-Folkestone-Ramsgate train, comprising eleven bogies (367 tons tare, 410 tons full) and hauled by Bulleid Pacific No.34066 SPITFIRE, did not actually leave Cannon Street until 6.07pm. At 6.20pm, a little over 5½ miles into its journey, some 140yds past St.Johns Station, it was travelling at approximately 30mph when it collided with the rear of a ten-coach electric passenger train (the 5.18pm Charing Cross-Hayes, running 30mins late), which was standing at the Parks Bridge Junction home signal. The air brakes of the electric train had been applied to hold it stationary on the rising gradient, and this resulted in the shock of the collision being even more severe than it otherwise would have been. Indeed, the underframe and body of the ninth coach were forced over and through the eighth coach, which was destroyed. Overall, the length of the train was reduced by 85ft.

In the Ramsgate train, the sudden stoppage resulted in the rear of the tender and the front of the leading coach being crushed together and thrown to the left. The 'jack-knifing' effect caused the tender and carriage to be thrown against the central steel column of the bridge which carried the Nunhead-Lewisham double line over the main line. The bridge column was thrown forward by some 20ft, and two of the bridge girders collapsed on to the Ramsgate train. They completely destroyed the leading coach of the train, and severely crushed the second coach and the front half of the third. Both trains were very heavily loaded

After emerging from Swindon Works in September 1957, the first double chimney 9F, No.92178, underwent a series of tests between Reading and Stoke Gifford. It is seen near Winterbourne. Note that No.92178 has had its smoke deflector plates removed, and note also the WR's vintage dynamometer car immediately behind the locomotive. PHOTOGRAPH: IVO PETERS

– a consequence of the disruption to rail services due to the fog. It was estimated that there were nearly 1,500 passengers in the electric train and 700 in the Ramsgate train. Inevitably, the toll was very high indeed. Altogether, 90 people were killed (89 passengers and the guard of the electric train), 109 were seriously injured, and 67 others sustained minor injuries or shock. Of those who were killed, it was possible to confirm that 39 had been travelling in the electric train and 49 in the Ramsgate train (in two cases such confirmation was impossible), the high fatality rate in the Ramsgate train being largely due to the bridge collapsing on to the leading coaches. It could have been even worse. A few moments after the accident the 5.22pm eight-coach Holborn Viaduct-Dartford electric train (also running very late) was about to cross over the bridge, but the driver spotted the girders at an odd angle and managed to bring his train to a halt. The leading coach was tilted, but the train was neither derailed nor damaged.

The official enquiry into the accident was very thorough (the report ran to 26 pages). It was soon ascertained that the signalling had been in proper working order at the time of the accident and that the brakes of the Ramsgate train had been fully operational. With those two possible causes ruled out, attentions were turned to the likelihood of human error. The driver of the Ramsgate train readily admitted that he had failed to observe two distant signals at 'Double Yellow' and 'Yellow', and was therefore totally unprepared for having to stop at the St.Johns inner home signal - indeed, on observing the inner home at 'Red', he hardly had time to apply the brakes before his train collided with the stationary electric train 138yds beyond the signal. The damning conclusion of the reporting officer was that '...I hold the driver solely responsible for the accident'.

The driver's failure to see the two distant signals was considered inexplicable; he had been a railwayman for 45 years and had been a driver for 18 years (with 13 years experience with the lightweight Pacifics) and was described by his supervisors at Ramsgate shed as having a 'thorough knowledge of the Eastern Section main line', and being 'reliable and sober' and a 'loyal and conscientious worker'. With his route knowledge, the driver was clearly aware that the signals were on the right-hand side of the line, and that the view of the signals from the driving position (on the left-hand side) would be obstructed at close range by the boiler casing. It would have been expected that, in the prevailing conditions of poor visibility, the driver would either have crossed to the other side of the cab or told his fireman to

look out, but he did neither. The inspecting officer speculated that the driver had not appreciated how severely the visibility was reduced and, possibly, that the driver – quite unjustifiably – felt that he would not be stopped at the inner home as he had never been stopped there before. It was indeed possible that the driver was unaware of just how bad the visibility actually was, as his fireman – also an experienced man with a good route knowledge – decided to make up the fire for the ascent to Knockholt rather than pay extra attention to the signals.

The driver of the Ramsgate train was tried for manslaughter on 21 April 1958. The jury disagreed, and at the second trial on 8 May he was acquitted. In some quarters, it was considered that the driver had suffered enough – he sustained such severe shock that, although the accident occurred on 4 December, he was not in a fit state to be interviewed by the inspecting officer until 10 January. The driver was still suffering from shock when he gave further evidence on 21 May – five and a half months after the accident.

During the investigation into the causes of the accident, various other factors – indeed, *all* relevant factors – were routinely taken into account. It was acknowledged that the stopping of the Hayes electric train at the St.Johns signal was unusual, but that train had been following a Hastings diesel-electric train, which itself had been detained for a long time by signals. But, unexpected stoppages or not, the stationary Hayes train had been fully protected by signals at the time it had been struck by the Ramsgate train. As for the visibility at the time of the accident, the ¾ mile-long section of line from New Cross station to St.Johns station was in a fairly deep cutting, and it was estimated that the visibility on this section was no greater than 30yds. The driver of a steam train which had passed through this section shortly before the accident confirmed that, even with the smaller Schools class 4-4-0 which he was driving, he had been unable to observe the St.Johns signals from the driving position and, therefore, had relied on his fireman to observe them. For some unknown reason, the driver of the Ramsgate train had not done likewise.

The reporting officer opined that the accident would almost certainly have been prevented by Automatic Train Control. It had been estimated that during the 46 years from 1912 to 1957, 31% of the fatalities in train accidents might have been avoided had ATC been in use. But, as mentioned earlier, it was 1956 before the go-ahead was given for equipping all Britain's main lines with ATC. On the Southern Region, it was proposed that the Western Section would be the first to be equipped with ATC, with the

Eastern Section being equipped later. It was considered that there was less urgency on the Eastern Section because of, firstly, the use of colour light signalling and, secondly, the widespread use of electric train sets which had the advantage of excellent visibility from the driving position.

Another point which came under discussion was the visibility from the cab of a Battle of Britain class engine. It was pointed out that the original engines of this type had cabs which were only 8ft 6in wide – a requirement of the Hastings line gauge – and the windscreen in the cab was therefore narrow. The report into the St.Johns accident endorsed the fitting of wider cabs and wider windscreens when the engines were being rebuilt. Inevitably, mention was made of the overbridge which had collapsed when struck by the Ramsgate train. However, no criticism was made of the design of the bridge – it had been erected as recently as 1929 – as the knock-on effect of the trains colliding was considered to have been something of a freak 'one-off'

The intensity of the accident was emphasised by the fact that the main line could not be reopened until the morning of 12 December – some 7½ days after the accident. The Nunhead-Lewisham line overhead was not reopened until 13 January and, even then, the replacement bridge was only temporary. Inevitably, the accident caused massive disruption to train services in the area, but although the main line passenger services returned to normal on 12 December, the continuing closure of the Nunhead-Lewisham line greatly affected the freight working at Hither Green. Until the reopening of that line, much of the Kentish traffic was re-routed via Redhill and Paddock Wood, thereby avoiding Hither Green completely. The isolation of Hither Green resulted in a number of ER and LMR lomotives being temporarily stranded there, but three 4F 0-6-0s and an 8F 2-8-0 managed to escape via Orpington and Bromley South on Sunday 8 December.

29.12.57: The former M&GN shed at Spalding was transferred from the New England district (where it had been a sub of 35A) to the Lincoln district, to become a sub of Boston (40F). At the time of the switch, Spalding's allocation comprised 14 steam locos and one diesel: Nos.11160, and 43059, 43061, 43062, 43064, 43065, 43080, 43083, 43085, 64171, 64172, 64191, 64207, 64231 and 64278.

30.12.57: A visit to Darlington Works prompted the observation that '...the scrapyard presented a heartbreaking sight, containing no fewer than seventeen engines...'. How times were to change. Within seven or eight years, the scrap sidings at the major works usually accommodated rather more than seventeen engines.

AROUND THE REGIONS IN 1957
The Western Region

Above. A Hall 4-6-0 on a mixed freight – this was a very common sight throughout the Western Region in the 1950s, but not always something which attracted the attention of photographers. We're happy to redress the balance with Gloucester shed's No.5907 MARBLE HALL on a mixed freight at Neath in June 1957. PHOTOGRAPH: P.F.WINDING

Below. Throughout the class's life, the 5101 2-6-2Ts were always well represented in the Wolverhampton Division, being used on all sorts of suburban and secondary passenger workings until their eventual displacement by DMUs. In May 1957, No.5185 of Leamington shed waits at Olton with what is presumably a Birmingham-Leamington local. PHOTOGRAPH: NEVILLE STEAD COLLECTION

You'll Remember those Black and White Days...

Above. Classic Western – and we're not referring to a John Wayne movie... On 16 April 1957, No.6001 KING EDWARD VII takes the 1.10pm Paddington-Birkenhead under Westbourne Bridge. No.6001 was a Stafford Road engine – it had been allocated there since 1954 and was, in fact, to see out its days there. By 1957 it had covered over 1,800,000 miles, and in the course of the year it underwent two unclassified repairs at Stafford Road and a light intermediate at Swindon. PHOTOGRAPH: R.C.RILEY

Below. On 3 July 1957, Collett 14XX 0-4-2T No.1470 of Newton Abbot shed heads towards Totnes on the main line, hauling the turnover auto trailer for the Ashburton branch. No.1470 spent all of its 26-year life in the Newton Abbot Division, being withdrawn from Exeter shed in October 1962. It was subsequently saved for preservation, one of four 14XXs to be rescued. PHOTOGRAPH: R.C.RILEY

The Beginning of the End

The 2,269th and last steam locomotive built at Darlington Works was Standard Class 2 2-6-2T No.84029, which was completed on 11 June 1957. PHOTOGRAPH: NATIONAL RAILWAY MUSEUM (DAR130)

During 1957 – the tenth year of BR's corporate existence – no fewer than five of its major workshops completed their last steam locomotives with varying degrees, or even a complete lack, of ceremony. The extent to which Britain's railways had built their own locomotives and rolling stock was exceptional when compared

by Philip Atkins

to other countries, and it was a tradition which had begun more than a century before British Railways came into existence in 1948. Over twenty railway-owned works in Britain built

locomotives early in the twentieth century, but after World War II just nine were thus engaged. Gorton Works in Manchester called it a day after erecting ten Thompson B1 4-6-0s during 1948/49, but continued to build Bo-Bo electric locomotives for the Manchester-Sheffield (via Woodhead) route into the early 1950s. Strangely,

No.84029 was also the last new steam locomotive to be delivered to the Southern Region. It was initially allocated to Ramsgate, and was photographed in late Summer 1957 on Blacksole Bank with a Faversham-Ramsgate train. PHOTOGRAPH: NATIONAL RAILWAY MUSEUM

Standard Class 4 2-6-0 No.76114 claimed the dubious distinction of being the last of 2,228 steam locomotives to be constructed at Doncaster Works. It emerged from the works for its formal portrait on 14 October 1957; in the centre of the group is BR's general manager, Gerald Fiennes.

the newest works of all – Eastleigh, established in 1910 – ceased as early as 1950 after assembling four Bulleid 'West Country' 4-6-2s, whereas the relatively cramped century-old Brighton Works was selected to design *and* build some of the forthcoming BR Riddles Standard steam locomotives.

In addition to designing the Class 9F 2-10-s (including the Crosti boiler variants) and the Class 4 4-6-0s and 2-6-4Ts, Brighton actually built no fewer than 130 of the Class 4 tanks over a period of six years. The last of these, BR No.80154, was despatched, entirely without ceremony, on 20 March 1957 and was uniquely accorded from new the recent British Transport Commission emblem in place of the 1949 'lion and wheel' device. As the last of 1,211 locomotives to have been built at Brighton over a period of 105 years, No.80154 could trace direct descent from the prototype Fowler LMS 2-6-4T No.2300, built thirty years earlier. Interestingly, the Fowler, Fairburn and Riddles 2-6-4Ts totalled exactly 800 engines, to which should be added 18 further derivatives in Ulster. All were in service during 1958, but scrapping of the Fowler engines began in 1959 and of the still fairly new Riddles engines as early as 1962. No.80154 succumbed at Nine Elms just after its tenth birthday in April 1967, never having received a

Minus the group – No.76114 fresh ex-works in October 1957.

No.76114 again – this time in later years at Corkerhill. **PHOTOGRAPH: B.P.HOPER COLLECTION**

Heavy General and still retaining its original boiler, an observation which applied to most post-1956 BR Standards. Within weeks of No.80154's completion at Brighton, part of the works was turning out Isetta bubble cars. In 1964 it closed completely, and has since been demolished.

Moving north, on 11 June 1957 Darlington Works outshopped BR Standard Class 2 2-6-2T No.84029 with a modicum of ceremony. It was the last of 2,269 steam locomotives to have been built there since 1864. The works continued to build diesel locomotives until 1964 – in June of that same year, incidentally, No.84029 was condemned at Wellingborough; it was just seven years old. On the steam front, Darlington built new boilers until late 1962 and continued to overhaul steam locomotives until September 1965. Complete closure on 2 April 1966 roughly coincided with the demise of neighbouring Robert Stephenson & Co, latterly part of the English Electric Co; this was a dual bitter blow to the local community, from which it has never fully recovered.

Only two days after the emergence of No.84029 from Darlington, Derby Works despatched – seemingly without any ceremony whatsoever – BR Caprotti Standard Class 5 4-6-0 No.73154, which was only five short of being the works' 3,000th steam

locomotive. Construction had commenced there in 1851, eleven years after the works had been established. Derby overhauled its final steam locomotive in September 1963, but continued to build diesels until 1967 and repair them until 1988. No.73154, which had also been accorded the new BTC emblem, was condemned at Motherwell in December 1966, but certain other BR and LMS Class 5 4-6-0s, which collectively totalled a remarkable 1,014 engines, saw out the steam era on BR in early August 1968.

The average life of the BR Standard steam locomotives was only a fraction of their theoretical economic life, not least those of the Class 4 2-6-0s which were, to a great extent, a rather 'tidied-up' version of the LMS Ivatt 'austerity' 2-6-0s. Just as some of the latter were built at Darlington after Nationalisation, several of the BR variety were constructed at Doncaster. No.76114 was photographed with works officials seated before it on 17 October 1957 – it was the 2,228th and last steam locomotive to be built at the plant, ninety years after the completion of its first Stirling 0-4-2. Doncaster Works continued to repair steam locomotives until 1963, even building new boilers for LNER Pacifics until 1961, and built diesel locomotives until 1987. No.76114, incidentally, was retired at Beattock in December 1966. On 29 November 1957 Horwich Works

completed 2-6-0 No.76099, its last steam locomotive. The works constructed 350hp diesel shunters until 1962. Steam repairs ceased in 1964, and the works finally closed in 1982, almost a century after it had been established, during which time it was credited with building 1,840 steam locomotives. No.76099 was condemned at Annesley in August 1966 after a life of less than nine years.

After 1957, Crewe and Swindon Works continued to build 9F 2-10-0s for a year or so, the final honours going to Swindon in March 1960 with the completion of No.92220 EVENING STAR. Between 1850 and 1950 British railway workshops built between them an average of one new steam locomotive every day, even though their prime purpose was actually carrying out repairs. Although the self-sufficiency of Britain's railways as regards steam locomotive construction was exceptional, their capability to build *diesel* locomotives, especially of the main-line variety, over a period of forty years was actually unique. Now, in turn, that era has effectively ended and the locomotive works of former years have all but disappeared. Their sites are now often occupied by supermarkets and car parks, which make it difficult to imagine the century or so of intense activity which they witnessed, even well within living memory.

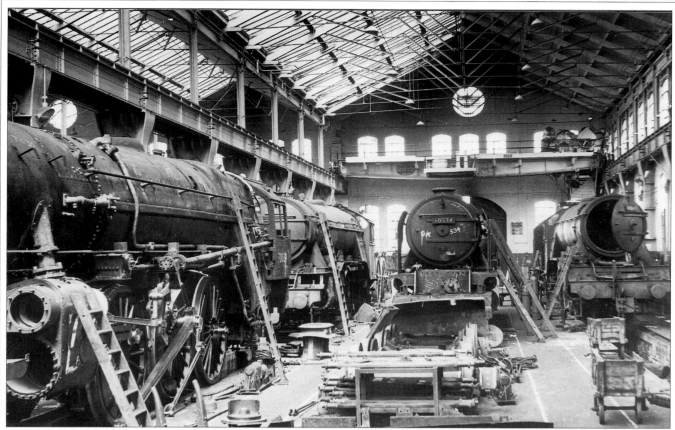

Despite the cessation of steam locomotive construction at Doncaster in 1957, the works continued to overhaul and repair steam locomotives for a few more years. As is clearly evident here, the repair shops were busy on 23 May 1959; from the left we have Britannia No.70039 SIR CHRISTOPHER WREN, A3 Pacific No.60107 ROYAL LANCER, A2 No.60534 IRISH ELEGANCE and A3 No.60064 TAGALIE. PHOTOGRAPH: BRIAN MORRISON

Brighton Works ceased the construction of steam locomotives in 1957, the last to be built there being Standard Class 4 2-6-4T No.80154 which was completed on 20 March. Locomotive work ceased completely at Brighton in 1958, bringing to an end a 106-year history. Only a few years previously – on 2 October 1954 – LMS diesel-electric No.10000 was photographed receiving attention in the works, while Standard Class 4 No.80094 was under construction. PHOTOGRAPH: BRIAN MORRISON

FOURUM – DELTIC in 1957
Notes by Reginald Rumbelow

RECORD COPY

DELTIC burst upon an unsuspecting enthusiast (and engineering) world in 1955. As we all knew – and if we didn't, the railway press soon told us – it was 'the most powerful single unit diesel in the world'. Moreover it was a private venture, a sort of showcase for the manufacturers, and BR's role was simply to provide the proving ground. DELTIC, based in Liverpool near its home, began trials in November 1955 and made its first trip to London later that month, with an Edge Hill to Camden freight. By 1957 the 'Ice Cream Cart' had firmly established itself on the London Midland Region, though over on the East Coast, far itchier fingers were waiting to get at it... It took as its own some of the best Liverpool-London trains, including The Shamrock (on which it first replaced an Edge Hill Pacific on 13 December 1955), The Manxman and The Merseyside Express. Above, the 'Goliath' (as Gerald Fiennes called it) runs in north of Stafford in 1957 and below, strains at the leash to get away from Crewe, back home to Liverpool.

DELTIC went to many places, and in various trials on the East Coast lost bits of its peripheral anatomy, knocked off a few sundry platform coping stones, and reorganised some of the signalling at Kings Cross. Despite Doubting Thomases, it was soon pronounced fit to test the revolutionary timetable then taking shape in the management mind of the Eastern, North Eastern and Scottish Regions. Quite why the London Midland felt unable to make further use of this awesome machine is not clear - it may have been looming electrification, but electrification was also very much on the cards for the East Coast. Before going to York in January 1959, DELTIC had some further wanderings to do: above sees it at Glasgow Central, taking the Canadian Trade Mission back to Manchester on 4 December 1957 and below at Longhedge in south London, hauling the then new EE Type 1 D8000, presumably bound for the 'Modern Travel Exhibition' at Battersea Wharf. LOWER PHOTOGRAPH: J.J.SMITH

Open and closed

During the 1950s the BR network underwent a slight contraction, with a few lines having their services withdrawn and some stations being closed. Although the closures were sometimes controversial and often contested, the scale was nothing compared with what was to follow in the 1960s.

Passenger stations opened/reopened:

28.1.57: Baildon (NER), between Bradford and Ilkley – reopened; had been closed since 5.1.53. The first train to stop there on reopening day was the 7.08am Skipton-Bradford, hauled by 2-6-0 No.43113, which picked up six passengers.

25.3.57: Acrow halt (ER), between Saffron Walden and Bartlow; built by Messrs Acrow Ltd at their own expense, principally for the benefit of their staff.

8.6.57: Scale Hall halt (LMR), between Lancaster (Green Ayre) and Morecambe.

30.9.57: Butlers Lane (LMR), a temporary station serving a new housing estate between Four Oaks and Blake Street stations on the Birmingham-Lichfield line.

Services withdrawn and lines closed:

1.2.57: Tewkesbury-Tewkesbury Quay (WR). Goods branch only.

1.2.57: Worcester (Foregate Street)-Worcester (Racecourse) (WR). Goods branch only – this was the well-known 'Butts Branch'. During the war, on-loan LNER J25 0-6-0s had been used on the branch.

4.3.57: Chesterfield (Market Place)-Arkwright Town (ER). The closure affected only goods traffic – passenger services into Chesterfield (Market Place) had been withdrawn as from 3 December 1951.

1.6.57: Cwmbach Jctn-Cwmbach Colliery (WR). Mineral branch only.

3.6.57: Elm Bridge-Abbeydore (WR); this was part of the celebrated Golden Valley Railway (Pontrilas to Hay-on-Wye) which had lost its passenger services in December 1941. The line had remained open for goods, but had been truncated at Dorstone in January 1950; it had been further truncated at Abbeydore in February 1953. Despite the closure of the Elm Bridge-Abbeydore section in 1957, the stub to Elm Bridge – where there was a Ministry of Supply depot – remained operational until March 1969.

1.7.57: Princes Risborough-Watlington (WR). Passenger services withdrawn, but the branch remained open for goods. Intermediate stopping places:

The Princes Risborough-Watlington branch closed to passengers as from Monday 1 July 1957, but in the absence of a Sunday service the last ordinary passenger trains ran on Saturday 29 July. With a conspicuous lack of 'last day' crowds at Chinnor on the Saturday, 0-6-0PT No.5755 approaches with a Watlington train. Despite the withdrawal of passenger services in 1957, the branch remained open for goods for a little longer and, happily, part of the line was eventually saved for preservation. PHOTOGRAPH: HUGH DAVIES COLLECTION

Left. **Acrow halt, a little to the north of Saffron Walden, was opened on 25 March 1957. The halt was constructed by Messrs.Acrow's and, as can be seen in the photograph, the station name-board was in Acrow's house style.**

Bledlow Bridge halt, Wainhill, Chinnor, Kingston Crossing halt, Aston Rowant, Lewknor Bridge halt.

1.7.57: Grimsargh-Whittingham Hospital. This was a private line which had opened in 1888 to connect Whittingham Hospital to the LNW/ L&Y Preston-Longridge branch at Grimsargh.

20.8.57: Warboys-Ramsey East (ER). This closure affected only private goods traffic – passenger services had been withdrawn from the Ramsey East branch on 22 September 1930, and on 17 September 1956 the section between Warboys and Ramsey had been taken over by Messrs.Cordells as a private siding.

2.9.57: Gowerton South-Llanmorlais (WR). Closed completely; passenger traffic had ceased in January 1931. Intermediate station: Penclawdd.

16.9.57: Waverton-Whitchurch (WR). Remained open to goods. Intermediate stations: Tattenhall, Broxton, Malpas.

16.9.57: Bentley-Bordon (SR). Remained open to goods and also to provide access at Bordon to the Longmoor Military Railway. Intermediate stopping place: Kingsley halt.

1.10.57: Trentham-Trentham Gardens (LMR). Closed to all traffic. The intermittent branch service (to Trentham Park, as it was originally known) was withdrawn in September 1927, reinstated (this time for summer Sundays only) in 1935, withdrawn again in 1939, and reinstated again on 7 October 1946 (with the branch terminus being renamed Trentham Gardens). During the last summer of operation – 1957 – there were frequent excursions to Trentham Gardens from the Birmingham area, usually on Sundays but occasionally mid-week. Although the branch wasn't officially closed until 1 October 1957, it is believed that the last excursion trains actually used the branch on 31 August.

30.12.57: Alne-Easingwold. Closed completely *(see separate feature)*.

30.12.57: Burghead-Hopeman (ScR). Closed completely. Passenger services on the entire Alves-Hopeman branch had been withdrawn on 14 September 1931, but the branch remained open for goods traffic. Since the early 1950s the section beyond Burghead had been worked only as required, and so it is uncertain when the last goods train actually ran on that section.

Passenger stations closed (in addition to those affected by the service withdrawals listed above):

7.1.57: Pant Glas (LMR) between Pen-y-Groes and Brynkir

7.1.57: Upwey Wishing Well halt, Monkton & Came halt (WR), both between Dorchester and Weymouth

4.2.57: Crowden (ER) between Woodhead and Hadfield

4.2.57: Grimston (LMR) between Melton Mowbray and Nottingham

4.2.57: Ordsall Lane (LMR) between Manchester and Eccles

4.2.57: Pont Lawrence halt (LMR) between Newport (Mon) and Tredegar

4.3.57: Stamford East (ER) - passenger services diverted to Stamford Town

1.4.57: Braunston & Willoughby (ER) between Rugby and Brackley

6.8.57: Lea (ER) near Gainsborough

The Llanmorlais branch diverged from the Central Wales line at Gowerton, a little to the north-west of Swansea. The branch lost its passenger services in 1931, but remained open to goods traffic until 2 September 1957. By this time, it had come under Western Region auspices, hence the apparition of a WR 'matchbox' at Penclawdd with the 11.20am goods from Gowerton South on 2 August 1957. PHOTOGRAPH: HUGH DAVIES

6.8.57: Newsholme (LMR) between Hellifield and Chatburn
16.9.57: Nursling (SR) between Redbridge and Romsey (It was reported that, on 9 December, the 7.25am Romsey-Southampton stopped there in error!)
16.9.57: Winson Green (LMR) on the Birmingham Stour Valley line

16.9.57: Brinklow, Shilton (LMR) both on Rugby-Nuneaton line
16.9.57: Hornby (LMR) between Lancaster and Skipton
16.9.57: Marchington (LMR) between Derby and Uttoxeter
16.9.57: Newsholme (LMR) between Blackburn and Hellifield
16.9.57: Stairfoot (ER) near Barnsley

(closed to regular pass traffic)
16.9.57: Hougham (ER) closed completely (between Newark and Grantham)
16.9.57: Claypole (ER) closed to passengers (between Newark and Grantham)
16.9.57: Methley North (NER) near Leeds

Thorney was one of three stations on the Peterborough-Sutton Bridge section of the old Midland & Great Northern which closed to passengers on 2 December 1957. Have *you* used Pears...?

Heaton Mersey shed was transferred to the jurisdiction of the Midland Division of the LMR on 1 January 1957, and was recoded 17E. In 1958 it underwent another change of code, this time to 9F. As an unashamed slice of nostalgia, how many of us remember following the directions given in Fl/Lt. Aidan Fuller's fabled Locoshed Directory: *'From Stockport Edgeley station... Go straight ahead outside the station along Station Road and turn left into Wellington Road. Descend the flight of steps into Mersey Square, and poroceed along Chestergate in a westerly direction. Continue along Brinksway and Stockport Road for about a mile. Turn right into Gorsey Bank*

Road and a cinder path leads from the right-hand side across a river to the shed. Walking time 30 minutes'. It seemed as if every shed in the land was reached by means of a cinder path – shed-bashing has never been the same since concrete paths were laid. And what about the 'walking times' quoted in the Directory? Fl/Lt.Fuller never seemed to take account of what Woodbines could do to teenage lungs – some of his 30-minute walks seemed very optimistic indeed.
PHOTOGRAPH: P.B.BOOTH; NEVILLE STEAD COLLECTION

16.9.57: Church Road halt (WR) between Bassaleg and Machen
14.10.57: Evenwood (NER) between Bishop Auckland and Barnard Castle
4.11.57: Sandal (ER) between Wakefield and Nostell
4.11.57: Thorington (ER) between Great Bentley and Alresford
2.12.57: Eye Green, Thorney, Wryde (ER) all on MGN - to passengers

Stations renamed:
4.3.57: LMR – Melton Mowbray (Midland) became Melton Mowbray (Town)
4.3.57: LMR – Corby & Weldon became Corby
16.9.57: WR – Cifrew became Cifrew halt
30.9.57: SR – Malden became New Malden

Engine sheds - divisional changes
On 1 January 1957 most of the London Midland Region engine sheds in the Leeds and Wakefield Districts were transferred to the North Eastern Region. The 541 locomotives allocated to the sheds at the time of transfer became NER stock. The sheds involved were recoded thus:
Leeds (Holbeck) – 20A to 55A
Stourton – 20B to 55B
Royston – 20C to 55D

Normanton – 20D to 55E
Manningham (sub: Ilkley) – 20E to 55F
Wakefield – 25A to 56A
Huddersfield – 25B to 55G
Goole – 25C to 53E
Mirfield – 25D to 56D
Sowerby Bridge – 25E to 56E
Low Moor – 25F to 56F
Farnley Junction – 25G to 55C

Also on 1 January 1957, an internal administrative shuffle on the LMR resulted in four of the one-time Cheshire Lines sheds being transferred to the Midland Division. They were:
Trafford Park (47 locos) – formerly 9E, recoded 17F
Heaton Mersey (56 locos) – formerly 9F, recoded 17E
Brunswick (33 locos) – 8E, code unchanged until 1958
Walton-on-the-Hill (19 locos) – 27E, code unchanged.

Following the aforementioned changes on 1 January 1957, the full list of BR shed codes was as follows (sub-sheds in brackets):
London Midland Region:
1A Willesden; **1B** Camden; **1C** Watford; **1D** Devons Road; **1E** Bletchley (Leighton Buzzard)
2A Rugby (Seaton); **2B** Nuneaton; **2C** Warwick; **2D** Coventry; **2E**

Northampton; **2F** Market Harborough
3A Bescot; **3B** Bushbury; **3C** Walsall; **3D** Aston; **3E** Monument Lane
5A Crewe North (Whitchurch); **5B** Crewe South; **5C** Stafford; **5D** Stoke; **5E** Alsager; **5F** Uttoxeter
6A Chester Midland; **6B** Mold Junction; **6C** Birkenhead; **6D** Chester Northgate; **6E** Wrexham Rhossdu; **6F** Bidston; **6G** Llandudno Junction; **6H** Bangor; **6J** Holyhead; **6K** Rhyl
8A Edge Hill; **8B** Warrington Dallam (Warrington Arpley); **8C** Speke Junction; **8D** Widnes (Widnes CLC); **8E** Brunswick; **8F** Warrington CLC
9A Longsight; **9B** Stockport Edgeley; **9C** Macclesfield; **9D** Buxton; **9G** Northwich
10A Wigan Springs Branch; **10B** Preston; **10C** Patricroft; **10D** Sutton Oak
11A Carnforth; **11B** Barrow (Coniston); **11C** Oxenholme; **11D** Tebay; **11E** * Lancaster
12A Carlisle Upperby; **12B** Penrith; **12C** Workington
14A Cricklewood; **14B** Kentish Town; **14C** St.Albans
15A Wellingborough; **15B** Kettering; **15C** Leicester Midland; **15D** Bedford
16A Nottingham; **16B** Kirkby-in-Ashfield; **16C** Mansfield
17A Derby; **17B** Burton (Horninglow, Overseal); **17C** Coalville;

Recoded on 1 January 1957 – Trafford Park shed became 17F, a consequence of an administrative reshuffle. The new code prevailed only until 1958, when it was recoded 9E. PHOTOGRAPH: ERIC SAWFORD

17D Rowsley (Cromford, Middleton, Sheep Pasture); **17E** Heaton Mersey (Gowhole); **17F** Trafford Park (Glazebrook)

18A Toton; **18B** Westhouses; **18C** Hasland; **18D** Staveley (Sheepbridge)

19A Sheffield; **19B** Millhouses; **19C** Canklow

20F * Skipton; **20G** * Hellifield

21A Saltley; **21B** Bournville; **21C** Bromsgrove

22A Bristol Barrow Road; **22B** Gloucester (Dursley, Tewkesbury)

24A Accrington; **24B** Rose Grove; **24C** Lostock Hall; **24D** Lower Darwen; **24E** Blackpool; **24F** Fleetwood; **24G** Skipton; **24H** Hellifield; **24J** Lancaster Green Ayre
26A Newton Heath; **26B** Agecroft; **26C** Bolton; **26D** Bury; **26E** Lees

27A Bank Hall; **27B** Aintree; **27C** Southport; **27D** Wigan L&Y; **27E** Walton-on-the-Hill

* The sheds marked with an asterisk were affected by an internal transfer which took place on 4 March, when the Lancaster, Settle and Carlisle lines were transferred from the Midland to the Central Division. The sheds affected were:
Skipton (30 locos) - formerly 20F, recoded 24G
Hellifield (15 locos) - formerly 20G, recoded 24H
Lancaster (35 locos) - formerly 11E, recoded 24J

Eastern Region:
30A Stratford (Chelmsford, Enfield Town, Epping, Walthamstow Wood St.); **30B** Hertford East (Buntingford); **30C** Bishops Stortford; **30E** Colchester (Braintree, Clacton, Maldon, Walton-on-Naze); **30F** Parkeston

31A Cambridge (Ely, Huntingdon East, Saffron Walden); **31B** March (Wisbech East); **31C** Kings Lynn (Hunstanton); **31D** South Lynn; **31E** Bury St.Edmunds (Sudbury)

32A Norwich Thorpe (Cromer Beach, Dereham, Wymondham); **32B** Ipswich (Aldeburgh, Felixstowe Beach, Stowmarket); **32C** Lowestoft; **32D** Yarmouth South Town; **32E** Yarmouth Vauxhall; **32F** Yarmouth Beach; **32G** Melton Constable (Norwich City)

33A Plaistow (Upminster); **33B** Tilbury; **33C** Shoeburyness

34A Kings Cross; **34B** Hornsey; **34C** Hatfield; **34D** Hitchin; **34E** Neasden (Aylesbury, Chesham)

35A New England (Spalding, Stamford); **35B** Grantham; **35C** Peterborough Spital Bridge

36A Doncaster; **36B** Mexborough (Wath); **36C** Frodingham; **36D** Barnsley; **36E** Retford (Newark)

38A Colwick (Derby Friargate, Leicester GN); **38B** Annesley; **38C** Leicester GC; **38D** Staveley; **38E** Woodford Halse

39A Gorton (Dinting, Hayfield)

40A Lincoln; **40B** Immingham (Grimsby, New Holland); **40D** Tuxford; **40E** Langwith Junction; **40F** Boston

41A Sheffield Darnall

North Eastern Region:
50A York; **50B** Neville Hill; **50C** Selby; **50D** Starbeck; **50E** Scarborough; **50F** Malton (Pickering); **50G** Whitby

51A Darlington (Middleton-in-Teesdale); **51B** Newport; **51C** West Hartlepool; **51D** Middlesborough; **51E** Stockton; **51F** West Auckland; **51G** Haverton Hill; **51H** Kirkby Stephen; **51J** Northallerton; **51K** Saltburn

52A Gateshead (Bowes Bridge); **52B** Heaton; **52C** Blaydon (Alston, Hexham); **52D** Tweedmouth (Alnmouth); **52E** Percy Main; **52F** North Blyth (South Blyth)

53A Hull Dairycoates; **53B** Hull Botanic Gardens; **53C** Hull Springhead (Alexandra Dock); **53D** Bridlington; **53E** Goole

54A Sunderland (Durham); **54B** Tyne Dock; **54C** Borough Gardens; **54D** Consett

55A Leeds Holbeck; **55B** Stourton; **55C** Farnley Junction; **55D** Royston; **55E** Normanton; **55F** Manningham (Ilkley); **55G** Huddersfield

56A Wakefield; **56B** Ardsley; **56C** Copley Hill; **56D** Mirfield; **56E** Sowerby Bridge; **56F** Low Moor; **56G** Bradford

Scottish Region:
60A Inverness (Dingwall, Kyle of Lochalsh); **60B** Aviemore (Boat of Garten); **60C** Helmsdale (Dornoch, Tain); **60D** Wick (Thurso); **60E** Forres

61A Kittybrewster (Ballater, Fraserburgh, Inverurie, Peterhead); **61B** Aberdeen Ferryhill; **61C** Keith (Banff, Elgin)

62A Thornton (Anstruther, Burntisland, Ladybank, Methil); **62B** Dundee Tay Bridge (Arbroath, Dundee West, Montrose, St.Andrews); **62C** Dunfermline (Alloa)

63A Perth South (Aberfeldy, Blair Atholl, Crieff); **63B** Stirling South (Killin, Stirling Shore Road); **63C** Forfar; **63D** Oban (Ballachulish)

64A St.Margarets (Dunbar, Galashiels, Longniddry, North Berwick); **64B** Haymarket; **64C** Dalry Road; **64D** Carstairs; **64E** Polmont; **64F** Bathgate; **64G** Hawick (Kelso, Riccarton, St.Boswells)

65A Eastfield (Arrochar); **65B** St.Rollox; **65C** Parkhead; **65D** Dawsholm (Dumbarton); **65E** Kipps; **65F** Grangemouth; **65G** Yoker; **65H** Helensburgh; **65I** Balloch; **65J** Fort William (Mallaig)

66A Polmadie; **66B** Motherwell; **66C** Hamilton; **66D** Greenock Ladyburn (Greenock Princes Pier)

67A Corkerhill; **67B** Hurlford (Beith, Muirkirk); **67C** Ayr; **67D** Ardrossan

68A Carlisle Kingmoor; **68B** Dumfries; **68C** Stranraer (Newton Stewart); **68D** Beattock; **68E** Carlisle Canal

Southern Region:

70A Nine Elms; **70B** Feltham; **70C** Guildford; **70D** Basingstoke; **70E** Reading; **70F** Fratton; **70G** Newport IoW; **70H** Ryde IoW

71A Eastleigh (Andover Junction, Lymington, Winchester); **71B** Bournemouth (Branksome); **71C** Dorchester; **71G** Bath S&D (Radstock); **71H** Templecombe; **71I** Southampton Docks; **71J** Highbridge

72A Exmouth Junction (Bude, Exmouth, Lyme Regis, Okehampton, Seaton); **72B** Salisbury; **72C** Yeovil Town; **72D** Plymouth Friary (Callington); **72E** Barnstaple Junction (Ilfracombe, Torrington); **72F** Wadebridge

73A Stewarts Lane; **73B** Bricklayers Arms; **73C** Hither Green; **73D** Gillingham; **73E** Faversham

74A Ashford (Canterbury West); **74B** Ramsgate; **74C** Dover (Folkestone); **74D** Tonbridge; **74E** St.Leonards

75A Brighton; **75B** Redhill; **75C** Norwood Junction; **75D** Horsham; **75E** Three Bridges; **75F** Tunbridge Wells West

Western Region:

81A Old Oak Common; **81B** Slough (Marlow, Watlington); **81C** Southall; **81D** Reading (Henley-on-Thames); **81E** Didcot; **81F** Oxford (Fairford)

82A Bristol Bath Road (Bath, Wells, Weston-super-Mare, Yatton); **82B** St.Philips Marsh; **82C** Swindon (Chippenham); **82D** Westbury (Frome); **82E** Yeovil Pen Mill; **82F** Weymouth (Bridport)

83A Newton Abbot (Ashburton, Kingsbridge); **83B** Taunton (Bridgwater); **83C** Exeter (Tiverton Junction); **83D** Laira (Launceston); **83E** St.Blazey (Bodmin, Moorswater); **83F** Truro; **83G** Penzance (Helston, St.Ives)

84A Stafford Road; **84B** Oxley; **84C** Banbury; **84D** Leamington Spa; **84E** Tyseley (Stratford-on-Avon); **84F** Stourbridge Junction; **84G** Shrewsbury (Builth Road, Clee Hill, Craven Arms, Knighton); **84H** Wellington; **84J** Croes Newydd (Bala, Penmaenpool, Trawsfynydd); **84K** Chester

85A Worcester (Evesham, Kingham); **85B** Gloucester (Brimscombe, Cheltenham, Cirencester, Lydney, Tetbury); **85C** Hereford (Ledbury, Leominster, Ross); **85D** Kidderminster

86A Ebbw Junction; **86B** Newport Pill; **86C** Cardiff Canton; **86D** Llantrisant; **86E** Severn Tunnel Junction; **86F** Tondu; **86G** Pontypool Road; **86H** Aberbeeg; **86J** Aberdare; **86K** Abergavenny (Tredegar)

87A Neath (Glyn Neath, Neath N&B); **87B** Duffryn Yard; **87C** Danygraig; **87D** Swansea East Dock; **87E** Landore; **87F** Llanelly (Burry Port, Pantyffynnon); **87G** Carmarthen; **87H** Neyland (Cardigan, Milford Haven, Pembroke Dock, Whitland); **87J** Goodwick; **87K** Swansea Paxton Street (Gurnos, Llandovery, Upper Bank)

88A Cardiff Cathays (Radyr); **88B** Cardiff East Dock; **88C** Barry; **88D** Merthyr (Cae Harris, Dowlais Central, Rhymney); **88E** Abercynon; **88F** Treherbert (Ferndale)

89A Oswestry (Llanidloes, Moat Lane); **89B** Brecon (Builth Wells); **89C** Machynlleth (Aberayron, Aberystwyth, Aberystwyth VoR, Portmadoc, Pwllheli)

On 4 March 1957 another divisional reshuffle on the LMR resulted in Hellifield shed being transferred to the Central Division and recoded 24H. After closure in 1963 the shed accommodated a number of preserved engines, but this reprise was fairly brief; the building was later abandoned and eventually demolished. PHOTOGRAPH: P.B.BOOTH; NEVILLE STEAD COLLECTION

You'll Remember those Black and White Days...

21 July 1957 at Cardiff Canton (86C); Britannia Pacific No.70026 POLAR STAR stands alongside the straight shed. Note the hand-holds cut into the smoke deflectors – these had replaced the original handrails, which had been blamed for a serious accident at Didcot in November 1955. PHOTOGRAPH: BRIAN MORRISON

Lancaster shed, the one-time Midland Railway depot at the west end of Green Ayre station, was recoded 24J in March 1957. The turntable seen here – a 60ft vacuum-operated model – had been installed in 1937. PHOTOGRAPH: P.B.BOOTH; NEVILLE STEAD COLLECTION

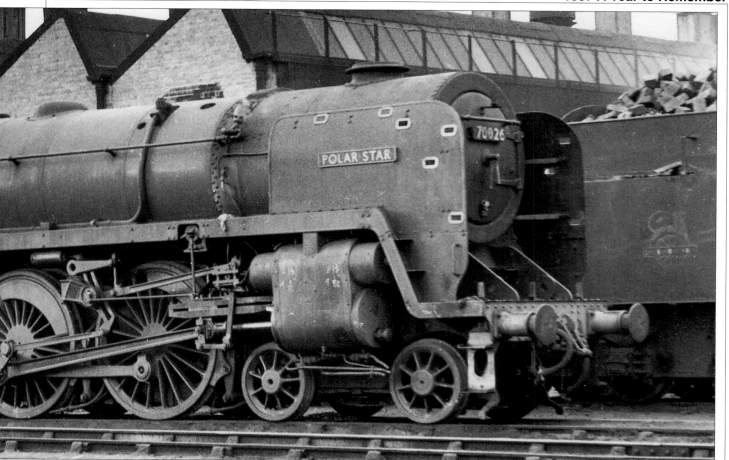

Dalry Road shed in Edinburgh was in the fork of the Princes Street-Dalry Road and Princes Street-Merchiston lines. In Caley and LMS days Dalry Road locos worked to Glasgow, Carstairs, Stirling and Perth, but by the 1950s the mainstay of work was local suburban duties, handled largely by Fairburn 2-6-4Ts. As the 1950s progressed, it became increasingly common to see ex-LNER types at Dalry Road – especially 0-6-0s and 0-6-2Ts. This picture was taken alongside the coal stage on 20 August 1957 - we have the old guard represented by ex-Caley 0-4-4T No.55165, while Jubilee 4-6-0 No.45663 JERVIS (clearly sporting the 22A shed-plate of Bristol Barrow Road!) is a less-than-commonplace visitor. PHOTOGRAPH: G.M.STADDON; NEVILLE STEAD COLLECTION

AROUND THE REGIONS IN 1957
The Southern Region

King Arthur 4-6-0 No.30454 QUEEN GUINIVERE passes Vauxhall with a Waterloo-Basingstoke train on 4 May 1957. The locomotive has an Drummond eight-wheel 'watercart' tender, but a couple of months after this picture was taken it received the Urie pattern tender from recently withdrawn N15 No.30755. PHOTOGRAPH: BRIAN STEPHENSON

Yes – this *is* the Southern Region...! A special troop train conveying the 2nd Battalion Scots Guards from Parkeston Quay to Victoria passes Longhedge Junction. The date is 27 February 1957. The leading B1 – No.61280 – had been attached at Channelsea Junction; the train engine is another B1, No.61375. PHOTOGRAPH: R.C.RILEY

1957 was the last full year the Britannias spent on the Southern. No.70014 IRON DUKE had come to the SR in June 1951 – when almost new – and after a three-month stint at Nine Elms it had moved to Stewarts Lane. It remained on Stewarts Lane's books until June 1958 when, along with the shed's other Britannias, it was transferred to Kentish Town. The highest-profile duty given to the Stewarts Lane Britannias was the Golden Arrow – on 27 February 1957, No.70014 is about to work the 'Arrow' to Dover. PHOTOGRAPH: R.C.RILEY

At the other end of the scale, B4 0-4-0T No.30096 shunts at Southampton Terminus – the date is 26 June 1957. The locomotive has a plated-in canopy-style cab with square spectacles – most of the class had round spectacles. No.30096 was the last B4 to be overhauled by BR, and after withdrawal in 1963, was sold to Messrs.Corrall's for use at Dible's Wharf at Southampton. It is now preserved. Three other B4s were based at Plymouth Friary in 1957, but were displaced by 204hp diesel shunters which arrived there in the Autumn – this brought the class's 65-year association with Plymouth to an end. PHOTOGRAPH: R.C.RILEY

Preservation

The preservation movement – as we know it today – blossomed in the late 1960s, but it should not be forgotten that preservationists were active in the 1950s. Indeed, by the time the first sections of BR line were privately purchased by enthusiasts in the 1960s, and by the time the first BR locomotives were being purchased from Barry, the folk involved with two famous narrow gauge lines in North Wales – the Festiniog and the Talyllyn Railways – had already notched up over a decade of experience in the fields of preservation and restoration.

Of the two narrow gauge lines, the Talyllyn was the first to be revived; it hadn't actually closed, although by the time the preservation society took over in 1951 the railway had been on its very last legs. By 1957, the Talyllyn was doing rather well. Partly due to BBC programmes about the railway in May of that year, public demand was such that the services had to

commence on 25 May instead of 1 June as had been advertised. During the summer season, most of the services were handled by No.3 SIR HAYDN and No.4 EDWARD THOMAS (an ex-Corris Railway engine), with No.6 DOUGLAS in reserve.

The other line, the Festiniog, had last been used by slate trains in 1946 (passenger services had ceased in 1939), and in 1954 a preservation society obtained the remnants of the old company. The new regime proudly recommenced passenger services between Portmadoc and Boston Lodge in July 1955. By 1957 the line had been extended to Penrhyndeudraeth, and plans were in hand for further extension to Tan-y-Bwlch. During the summer of 1957 0-4-0ST PRINCE (built by George England in 1864) and Fairlie-type 0-4-4-0T TALIESIN (Vulcan Foundry, 1876) were used in turn on the four daily trains in each direction. During August some 500 passengers were being carried daily,

and at the end of the season the FR could count the receipts from over 54,000 passengers – an increase of more than 15,000 over 1956.

The Talyllyn and Festiniog Railways were pioneers in the field of preservation and, as just reward for forty-plus years of enterprise, enthusiasm and perseverance, they are now hugely popular attractions.

Above. **On 29 September 1957 the Festiniog's superbly restored Fairlie 0-4-4-0T TALIESIN poses at Boston Lodge. PHOTOGRAPH: IVO PETERS**

Top right. **0-4-0ST PRINCE (with its four-wheeled tender) pulls Fairlie 0-4-4-0T MERDDIN EMRYS out of the engine shed for a photo-call on 29 September 1957. As betrayed by its general condition and sack-covered chimney, the Fairlie is still awaiting restoration. PHOTOGRAPH: IVO PETERS**

Having crossed the Cob from Portmadoc, PRINCE approaches Boston Lodge sheds on 29 September 1957. PHOTOGRAPH: IVO PETERS

Mensing in the Midlands

During 1957, photographer Michael Mensing was very active in and around the Birmingham area. This superb picture shows Compound No.41095 waiting to leave the gloom of Birmingham New Street on 16 May with the 1.45pm to Norwich, Yarmouth and Cromer; the train will travel via the Midland & Great Northern line. PHOTOGRAPH: MICHAEL MENSING

Compound No.41123 pulls away from Platform Nine of Birmingham New Street with the 5.45pm stopping train to Bristol on 6 May 1957. PHOTOGRAPH: MICHAEL MENSING

You'll Remember those Black and White Days...

Sunny Warwickshire, Sunday 2 June 1957 – Stanier 2-cylinder 2-6-4T No.42582 leaves Hampton-in-Arden with the 1.15pm Birmingham New Street-Coventry service. PHOTOGRAPH: MICHAEL MENSING

Across to the north-west, in rural Shropshire, Jubilee No.45587 BARODA has passed All Stretton Halt with the 7.30am Penzance-Manchester London Road on Whit Monday, 10 June 1957. Fortunately, this delightful line – via Hereford. Ludlow and Shrewsbury – is still very much with us. PHOTOGRAPH: MICHAEL MENSING

On 24 August 1957, the 9.30am Bournemouth West-Birkenhead has just passed Bentley Heath Crossing, near Knowle & Dorridge. No.1008 COUNTY OF CARDIGAN of Chester shed is in charge. PHOTOGRAPH: MICHAEL MENSING

Churchward's 43XX 2-6-0s were unsung heroes – despite performing a wide variety of duties, almost always with total satisfaction, they rarely had a share of the limelight. This Summer Saturday train – believed to be the 8.50am Margate-Birmingham Snow Hill – is well loaded, but the operating department would have had little hesitation in giving the turn to a trusty 43XX, in this case No.6379. The train has just passed Solihull station; the date is 10 August 1957. PHOTOGRAPH: MICHAEL MENSING

The 7.53pm Knowle & Dorridge-Birmingham Snow Hill leaves Widney Manor station, with 51XX 2-6-2T No.5106 in charge.
PHOTOGRAPH: MICHAEL MENSING

As if to complete a round trip and finish back in central Birmingham, 56XX 0-6-2T No.6609 climbs out of the tunnel and enters Snow Hill with a down goods on 7 November 1957. PHOTOGRAPH: MICHAEL MENSING

AROUND THE REGIONS IN 1957
London Midland

On Sunday 2 June 1957 the 10.40am Euston-Wolverhampton (H.L.) approaches Hampton-in-Arden station; Jubilee No.45647 STURDEE is in charge. The train has just rejoined the down line; because of permanent way works, single-line working (using the up line) had been in force for part of the way between Berkswell and Hampton. The train waiting to proceed on the up line is the 1.15pm Birmingham (New Street)-Coventry, headed by 2-6-4T No.42582, while 4F 0-6-0 No.44302 stands on the right, waiting its next pilot duty. PHOTOGRAPH: MICHAEL MENSING

You'll Remember those Black and White Days...

Standard 2-10-0 No.92026 was one of the ten class members to be fitted with a Crosti boiler, intended to reduce coal consumption by up to 19%. The anticipated saving did not materialise and, even more frustrating, the Crosti-fitted examples proved to be less powerful than the 'ordinary' 9Fs. Consequently, starting in 1959 they were converted for conventional operation. With just one brief exception, the ten Crosti examples spent the 1950s based at Wellingborough shed, where they were used principally on the iron ore trains. On 25 May 1957 No.92026 took a train of loaded hoppers back to Wellingborough; it is seen between Mill Hill Broadway and Elstree. Note that, in Crosti fashion, the exhaust is coming from the chimney alongside the firebox on the far side of the locomotive. PHOTOGRAPH: BRIAN MORRISON

In not-untypical Lakeland drizzle, Ivatt 2MT 2-6-2T No.41217 stands at Coniston. This attractive station must have been one of the most scenically-sited establishments in Britain. The date is given as 27 December 1957, but given the leaves on the trees we suspect it is a little earlier in the year. PHOTOGRAPH: P.B.BOOTH; NEVILLE STEAD COLLECTION

The state of play

The two LM main-line diesels, Nos.10000 and 10001, on the up Royal Scot at Lancaster. PHOTOGRAPH: RAY FARRELL

Throughout each year – during the 1950s, at least – the Railway Clearing House prepared monthly traffic reports. The reports were lengthy – usually around 40 pages for each month – and so it is obviously impracticable to include here all the details from every report for 1957. It is therefore hoped that a few random extracts from one month's report will suffice; much of it is routine fare, but it provides an insight into the day-to-day running of the vast industry that was British Railways. The report we have selected is the one for June 1957.

The overall picture was mixed. All classes of passenger traffic had increased, albeit partly due to the aftermath of petrol rationing (which had actually ended on 14 May), and partly because of the Whitsun holiday traffic (7-11 June). The interruption of the holiday period had, however, resulted in a drop in the volume of freight traffic and, furthermore, although certain categories of freight – especially minerals – had actually increased in volume, receipts from the same categories had fallen. To look after the £36.5million-worth of traffic

during the four-week period, BR employed 589,836 staff; compared to the same period in 1956 that was a £1.2million decrease in traffic, but an 8,399 increase in the number of staff.

On the motive power front, it was noted that '...five of the seven main line diesels were in service on most days' during the month in question. The actual figures were (see table bottom). The seemingly poor availability of Deltic was due largely to it having been on exhibition at Battersea for seven days. Of the two gas turbine locos in service, No.18000 spent eight days under repair during the relevant period (otherwise, it was working between Paddington and Bristol) while the Metro-Vick loco, No.18100, was reported to be 'still at the makers'.

On the multiple unit front, during the month under scrutiny six two-car sets had been delivered for the Durham County scheme, one two-car set for the Darlington-Saltburn scheme, and one for the Hull area. Also, lightweight diesel sets had been introduced on the Manchester-Marple-Macclesfield and Hayfield lines. On the Bradford-Leeds-Harrogate, the Newcastle-Carlisle, the Hull-Withernsea and the Hull-Hornsea routes, the diesel services had brought about an increase of between 4% and 14% in passenger receipts compared to the same period for 1956, while on the Leeds-Wakefield route the increase was a whopping 153%. On the Glasgow-Edinburgh route, where diesel units had been introduced at the start of 1957, figures were up by 24%.

A separate summary later in 1957 gave figures for LMR diesel services - these are listed in the accompanying table.

The report also made mention of negotiations with the Kraus Maffei Co of Munich for the construction, under licence, of 'V200' type diesel-hydraulic locomotives. As things turned out, the British-built versions – the Western Region's 'Warship' class – first appeared in August 1958. As for electric services, it was reported that work had commenced on the reconstruction of Mauldeth Road and East Didsbury stations in preparation for the electrification of the Manchester-Crewe line, while tenders were being sought for the conversion of 124 Southend line multiple units sets from 1500v DC to 25,000v AC.

Despite all the talk of diesel locomotives and multiple-units – the new era of British Railways, as it were - at a few locations certain shunting duties were still performed by horses. Some details are given in the accompanying table.

As for passenger traffic, among the special workings noted during the four-week period in 1957 were the Starlight Specials (St.Pancras-Edinburgh/Glasgow – nine trains during the four weeks), excursions from Leicester and Derby to Kensington (for the summer sales – one of the stores presented free luncheon vouchers to the passengers!), a Ramblers Association excursion from Manchester to Coniston, a special for the pupils of five East Lothian schools to Glasgow and thence on a Clyde

	Days In service	Days Out of service
No.10000	21	4
No.10001	18	7
No.10100	24	1
No.10201	7	7
No.10202	24	1
No.10203	24	1
No.10800	1	24
Deltic	13	12

In 1957 the LMR announced that more than 1¼ million passengers per month were travelling by its new diesel services. The figures were based on a survey conducted during October, and were compared with the figures for one month in 1956.

Services	Date Introduced	October 1957	One month 1956	Increase
West Cumberland Area	7.2.55	144,585	140,710	3,875
Watford-St.Albans	25.7.55	37,877	140,710	2,782
Bury-Bacup	6.2.56	101,614	92,688	8,926
Birmingham-Lichfield	5.3.56	275,508	159,603	115,905
North Wales Area	28.5.56	104,133	83,902	20,231
Banbury-Buckingham	13.8.56	6,423	2,693	3,730
Manchester-Buxton/Macclesfield	8.10.56	316,400	186,858	61,535
Manchester-Hayfield/Macclesfield	17.6.57	198,303	136,768	61,535
Harrow & Wealdstone-Belmont	6.8.57	889	397	492
Crewe-Stoke-Derby	16.9.57	84,248	60,154	24,094

cruise (1,132 passengers, £385 receipts), and a cyclists' excursion from Waterloo to Bournemouth (380 passengers plus bicycles, receipts £280). The forthcoming specials under discussion included the conveyance of the Royal Canadian Mounted Police – 39 personnel and 36 horses – to performances and demonstrations throught the country, and also a proposed repeat of a special train for the British Lambretta Association (Paddington to Taunton and back, scooters conveyed on the train – but wasn't the idea to *ride* the scooters?).

Regarding freight, the report commented on seasonal traffic: '...*movement of vegetables from the Channel Islands heavy, and 4,765 wagon loads dispatched from Weymouth and Southampton during the four weeks... Cornish seed potato traffic – 1,542 wagon loads during the four weeks... fruit from Brest commenced to pass via Plymouth – 404 vans by special and ordinary services...1,930 wagons of bananas by 30 special trains...*'.

The various longer-term traffic developments were also detailed. Among them were:

Oil: Motor spirit (an estimated 46,000 tons p.a.) and fuel oil (34,000

tons p.a.) traffic from Thames Haven and Purfleet respectively had been secured, both commodities going to a new depot at Northampton. An additional 25,000 tons of motor spirit and 15,000 tons of fuel and gas oil was expected to be taken by rail from Thames Haven to a new depot at Thame, in Oxfordshire.

Peas and beans: 1,000 tons of peas and beans from Messrs A.Brown of Epworth to Fraserburgh and 500/600 tons to Maidstone – traffic secured.

Appleby-Frodingham Steel Co of Scunthorpe: 3,000 tons of sheet steel piling for shipyard development at Newport (Mon). Traffic to be conveyed by rail.

Wine: Two glass-lined continental tank wagons of 'Dubonnet' from Ster in Southern France travelled via Dunkirk and Dover to Messrs.Roce & Co of St.Albans, and this was expected to be the start of a regular traffic of wine in bulk.

Cement: From the Tunnel Portland Cement Co at Tring to the Clyde Portland Cement Co in Glasgow.

Dross: Some 60,000 tons p.a. had been conveyed by rail from Addiewell to Braehead Power Station prior to 1956, but the traffic had been lost to road transport. However, during the period of petrol rationing the railways regained 50% of the traffic, and in 1957 it was anticipated that the remainder would also soon be regained.

Yarn: From Alloa to Kew Bridge – some 300/400 tons were switched to the railways during the petrol shortage, and BR secured this traffic permanently.

Beer: 650 tons-worth of beer from Robert Youngers of Edinburgh had previously been conveyed to Aberdeen by sea, but the traffic was secured by BR.

Chemicals: Special rates were agreed for the conveyance by rail of Styrene Monomer – 8,000 tons p.a. from

Grangemouth and 4,000 tons from Manchester – in private owner wagons to the International Synthetic Rubber Co's new factory at Fawley. Also, ICI had applied for a private siding from the Avonmouth-Severn Beach line to their proposed new factory.

Carbon Black: A pilot scheme was announced for the use of the 'Tote' bulk handling system for the transportation of carbon black from Avonmouth to Fort Dunlop. The method involved the use of special bins loaded through a top aperture and unloaded through a bottom discharge door, which could be hermetically sealed to protect the contents.

Astral telescope: A one-off consignment from Southall to the Vatican City, via BR and the Harwich-Zeebrugge ferry. (Honest!)

New and projected factories etc from which rail business may be expected: Esso Petroleum Co at Howdon-on-Tyne; new opencast coal site at Lochgelly; development of ICI site in Gloucestershire (nr. Avonmouth); expansion of opencast workings in the Banbury area; new dry dock at Swansea; new inter-store movement of RAF traffic.

..........ooo000ooo..........

On regal matters, in 1957 a new category of Royal train appeared. This was allotted the code word 'Deeplus', and encompassed the trains which carried VIPs in connection with Royal occasions. The two existing Royal train code words, 'Grove' and 'Deepdene', remained as before. Of those two categories, 'Grove', which was the name of the wartime headquarters at Watford, was reserved for the train carrying HM The Queen, while 'Deepdene', named after the wartime HQ at Dorking, was used for trains carrying other members of the Royal Family.

The working of 'Grove', 'Deepdene' and 'Deeplus' trains warranted a special 11-page book of instructions. Generally, the instructions were intended to ensure an uninterrupted passage of the train, partly for security purposes; for example, all shunting movements at intermediate stations had to be suspended for ten minutes prior to the passage of a 'Grove' train (five minutes for 'Deepdene'), guards of all trains which a 'Grove' train was scheduled to pass were required to '...*specially examine their loads...*', and no road vehicle '...*must be allowed to cross the line at any public level crossing for 15 minutes before the Special Train is expected to pass*'. Also at level crossings along the Royal

The Camden Area of the London Midland Region quoted the following numbers of '...horses bedded on straw' for 1957:

Location	1.1.57	31.12.57
St.Pancras Parcels	35	Nil
Kensington High Street	2	2
Camden Goods (at depot)	4	4
...ditto.. (delivery)	21	18
Hendon	2	Nil
Out to grass	5	Nil
TOTALS	69	24

Although not in any way relevant to the year of 1957, we couldn't resist this little snippet from the Great Northern Railway rulebook of 1912: '*Company's horses must not be allowed to take water (either on or off company's premises) at troughs which are used by horses belonging to the public. G.N. Horses requiring water when away from their stables must be watered at the company's nearest stable or receiving office, from buckets specially provided for this purpose, which buckets must be used exclusively for the company's horses*'.

Progress?

In the following tables, various financial statistics for 1957 are compared with the corresponding figures for the preceding year and also – for the purpose of longer-term comparison – for 1948. One particular point is very clear – although BR's gross revenue increased by almost 50% between 1948 and 1957, during that period an operating profit of over £26m turned into a loss of over £27m. It is clear that the biggest financial turn-around was evidenced on the Western Region, where a net profit of £834,000 for 1948 was turned into a deficit of over £20 million for 1957. This must have been one in the eye for the legion of GWR/WR devotees who thought that 'Gods Wonderful Railway' could do no wrong.

Another interesting point is the light engine mileages (deduct the 'total train miles' figures from the 'total engine miles' figures). Although there was a slight decrease in light engine mileage between 1948 and 1957, by the latter year almost one third of all engine miles were still run light. It was a remarkably high proportion. It will be noted that the only region with a well-below-average light engine mileage was the Southern, which returned a figure of just 12%. This, presumably, was a hark-back to the practices of the old Southern Railway which, rather than have an engine run light, would use it to double- or even treble-head a modestly loaded train.

	LMR £000	WR £000	SR £000	ER £000	NER £000	ScR £000	Total £000
(a) Gross Receipts							
1948	108,144 _32.17%_	54,776 _16.30%_	48,858 _14.53%_	56,743 _16.88%_	32,594 _9.70%_	35,021 _10.42%_	336,136
1956	148,937 _30.96%_	83,631 _17.39%_	56,063 _11.65%_	81,370 _16.92%_	63,397 _13.18%_	47,639 _9.90%_	481,037
1957	153,051 _30.52%_	86,562 _17.26%_	60,088 _11.99%_	84,538 _16.86%_	66,232 _13.21%_	50,959 _10.16%_	501,430
(b) Working Expenses							
1948	104,225 _33.63%_	54,142 _17.47%_	37,071 _11.96%_	55,187 _17.81%_	24,792 _8.00%_	34,461 _11.13%_	309,878
1956	145,937 _29.33%_	101,449 _20.39%_	59,587 _11.98%_	80,021 _16.08%_	55,731 _11.20%_	54,809 _11.02%_	497,534
1957	153,610 _29.06%_	106,631 _20.17%_	64,764 _12.25%_	85,390 _16.15%_	59,122 _11.18%_	59,154 _11.19%_	528,671
(c) Net Receipts							
1948	3,919	634	11,787	1,556	7,802	560	26,258
1956	3,000	-17,818	-3,524	1,349	7,666	-7,170	-16,497
1957	-559	-20,069	-4,575	-852	7,110	-8,195	-27,140
(d) Total Train Miles							
1948	107,516 _29.41%_	61,464 _16.81%_	63,106 _17.26%_	59,268 _16.21%_	29,078 _7.96%_	45,140 _12.35%_	365,572
1956	94,790 _25.21%_	67,314 _17.90%_	68,812 _16.30%_	63,730 _16.95%_	39,531 _10.51%_	41,841 _11.13%_	376,018
1957	94,441 _24.73%_	68,249 _17.67%_	69,731 _18.26%_	66,027 _17.29%_	40,242 _10.53%_	43,240 _11.32%_	381,930
(e) Total Engine Miles							
1948	164,241 _30.56%_	94,815 _17.64%_	76,807 _14.29%_	88,618 _16.49%_	43,286 _8.06%_	69,673 _12.96%_	537,460
1956	139,492 _26.45%_	98,220 _18.62%_	81,480 _15.44%_	88,624 _16.80%_	56,906 _10.79%_	62,757 _11.90%_	527,547
1957	138,492 _26.02%_	99,172 _18.64%_	82,273 _15.46%_	90,746 _17.05%_	57,137 _10.74%_	64,336 _12.09%_	532,156

route, '...where male Crossing Keepers are stationed the man in charge must be on duty, and at all level crossings which are in the charge of women, a competent man must be employed 30 minutes before the Special Train is due to pass...'. As for that last instruction, the year 1957 was, of course, a little before terms such as 'sexist' and 'politically correct' entered common parlance.

Not quite....
One particularly intriguing report surfaced in 1957. It demonstrated that railway history, like any other aspect of history, is full of 'might have beens'. In this category are the proposals – some of great intensity and with enthusiastic support – which failed to become reality. One particular railway 'might have been' is a main line connection to Heathrow Airport. The idea had been discussed, often in considerable depth, several times since World War II, and although Heathrow was eventually rail connected (in the late 1970s), the reality took the form of LT's Picadilly Line extension, rather than the Southern Railway or BR 'main line' which had featured in earlier proposals.

In 1954, the latest in the series of reports considered a railway service, provided by the Southern Region, from Waterloo '...to a point near Feltham whence a new line might be constructed to London Airport...', but the bottom line was that such a service would have to be heavily subsidised, and so the idea was dropped. However, in 1954/55 it was realised that the future volume of air traffic at Heathrow looked like substantially exceeding all expectations, and so a new report was commissioned. This was undertaken by the tediously titled 'Working Committee into the Rail Connection to London Airport', whose report was published in March 1957.

The report is fascinating – not least of all because it was not released to the public for thirty years! – but, with considerable reluctance, it has been decided to include only brief extracts here. The reason for this brevity...? It is simply that the railway which was proposed was never built.

In its report, the Working Committee recognised three alternative rail routes to Heathrow:

1) An SR route from London via a new line from Feltham; this was similar to the proposal of 1954 but, this

One of the new Derby-built DMU sets on trial near Bearley in Warwickshire, on 24 April 1957. The cars are W50050, 59000 and (we believe) 50092. PHOTOGRAPH: R.C.RILEY

TG/11/15/C.   14th March, 1957.

Dear Sir,

SALOON NO. 9006 -
Use of Electric Razor.
————————————

In connection with the recent journey of H.R.H.
The Prince Philip, Duke of Edinburgh, to Cheltenham
in Saloon 9006, the question of facilities for the
use of an electric razor was brought to notice. As a
temporary expedient the request in this case was met
by obtaining the transformer which is normally used in
the First Class Sleeping Car working in the 12.30am
Paddington to Penzance.

It is, however, desired that facilities should
always be available to enable an electric razor to be
used in Saloon 9006 and I should be grateful if you
would let me know quickly what can be arranged in this
respect.

Yours truly,

C.T.Roberts, Esq.,
SWINDON.

TG/11/15/C.
CW.117. RS.33.   16th May, 1957

Dear Sir,

SALOON NO. 9006 - Use of Electric Razor.
————————————

With reference to your letter of the 8th instant,
arrangements were made to use the transformer out of the
Sleeping Car working in the 12.30am Paddington to Penzance
for the journey of H.R.H. The Prince Philip when he
travelled to Coaley Junction in Saloon No. 9006 on
Tuesday night, May 14th. As you are aware, this
transformer is rather large and I should, therefore,
be glad if you would arrange to expedite the supply of
the smaller type rotary convertor.

When this is being fitted, will you kindly
arrange if practicable, for it to be concealed behind
the panelling in the berth so that only the socket
into which the razor fits is visible.

Perhaps you would be good enough to confirm that
this can be arranged.

Yours truly,

S.G. HEARN

per "L.W.I."

The case of the Royal razor. A further missive came from Swindon on 11 July, stating that '...it would be desirable to suppress the converter against radio interference'.

route was 16.7 miles in length.

The report referred to the anticipated growth of traffic at Heathrow Airport. At the time, the latest official estimate was that, by 1960, the airport would have to deal with 5.2million passengers (not a bad estimate – the actual figure for 1960 was 5.4million), and by 1970 the figure would be 11.5million (actual figure for 1972 – 18.7million). The proposed railway would have to cope with, not only a proportion of this traffic, but also a projected ½-million single journeys per annum undertaken by spectators, airport employees, and friends of airline passengers. The possibility of carrying freight – maintenance stores and aircraft fuel were cited – on the proposed railway was also considered.

In order to assess the possible profitability of a the proposed line, the committee had to address the matter of fares. Under the BTC charging scheme the 16.7-mile rail journey from Victoria to Heathrow would attract a fare of 2/8d (14p), but there were exemptions to the scheme. One such exemption was in the case of 'any train specially provided for any particular passengers or purposes' – the committee was confident that the airport services would fall into that category, and worked on the assumption that the single Victoria-Heathrow rail fare would be set at 5/- (25p). This was the same as the fare charged, at the time, by the road coaches between Heathrow and Earls Court terminal. With that fare in mind, the committee calculated that, by 1963, the railway to the airport would be generating annual receipts of £980,000, while by 1970 – by which date it was reckoned that the airport would be at maximum capacity – the annual revenue was estimated at over £1.5million.

As for services on the proposed line, it was agreed that a frequent service – preferably with an interval of only 10 minutes – was absolutely essential '...first, to avoid waiting times and, secondly, to avoid the arrival of passengers at London Airport in groups which would be inconveniently large for processing'. The estimated journey time was 25 minutes. The latest SR electric rolling stock was considered to be of a suitable standard for the services, but although four-coach trains would have seats for up to 400 passengers it was considered that the provision of luggage accommodation – rather essential on trips to and from a major international airport – would reduce the capacity of each train to a nominal 320. The report acknowledged that a new terminal would have to be built at the Victoria end, and three alternative schemes – each for a twin-track three-platform station were evaluated:

1) A low level station adjacent to the

time, Victoria was favoured as the terminal instead of Waterloo.

2) An extension of the existing LT line from Hounslow West '...but this would involve very expensive construction if an adequate and fast service for air passengers were to be provided'. (This scheme was, in fact, the basis of one which came to fruition in the 1970s).

3) A new line from the WR main line near Hayes & Harlington, but this was ruled out '...because the Paddington area was not considered by the Airways representatives to be acceptable for an in-town terminal'.

Clearly, the first of those three options was the favourite. The committee suggested that the route between Victoria and Feltham should be via Clapham Junction, Barnes, Kew Bridge and Hounslow rather than via Richmond and Twickenham (as had previously been suggested) – the Kew Bridge route was acknowledged as being slightly longer, but was preferred on operating grounds and, moreover '...the widening works required to adapt the Richmond line for the airport service would almost certainly be more costly than those required on the Hounslow line...'. Taking into account the proposed new line from Feltham to the central area of the airport, the

BRITISH RAILWAYS

IN CONJUNCTION WITH

The Ramblers' Association (Northern Area)

Conducted Rambles from Reedsmouth, Bellingham, Tarset, Kielder, Deadwater and Riccarton

(For routes see over)

Rambles available for individuals as well as organised parties
(Leaders provided)

SPECIAL RAMBLERS' EXCURSION TO

REEDSMOUTH, BELLINGHAM, TARSET, FALSTONE, KIELDER FOREST, DEADWATER, RICCARTON JCT. & HAWICK

SUNDAY 21st JULY

OUTWARD		SECOND CLASS RETURN FARES.								RETURN	
		Reeds-mouth	Bellingham	Tarset	Falstone	Kielder Forest	Dead-water	Riccarton Jct.	Hawick		
NEWCASTLE ...dep.	a.m. 9 30	s.d. 5/9	s.d. 6/3	s.d. 6/6	s.d. 7/3	s.d. 8/3	s.d. 8/3	s.d. 9/0	s.d. 10/9	Hawick ....dep. Riccarton Jct. .. Deadwater .... Kielder Forest .. Falstone .... Tarset .... Bellingham .... Reedsmouth .... NEWCASTLE arr.	p.m. 6 35 7 5 7 15 7 20 7 35 7 45 7 55 8 15 9 45
ARRIVAL TIMES		a.m. 11 6	a.m. 11 27	a.m. 11 34	a.m. 11 47	p.m. 12 5	p.m. 12 13	p.m. 12 25	p.m. 12 51		

LIGHT REFRESHMENTS WILL BE AVAILABLE IN EACH DIRECTION

TARIFF.

Tea	per cup 6d.	
Coffee	per cup 8d.	
Bovril or Oxo	per cup 8d.	
Bread & Butter	6d.	
Biscuits	per portion 4d.	
Chocolate	4d.	
Cake	per portion 6d.	
Cake/Pastries	each 6d.	

Sandwiches, per half round or rolls :—
Ham, Tongue .... 11d.
Pressed Meat/Galantine ... 9d.
Cheese, Egg, Cress, Tomato ... 8d.
Sausage Rolls .... 6d.
Pickles or Chutney per portion 6d.
Potato Crisps .... 4d.
Soup (with Roll or Bread) ... 1s. 0d.
Ice Cream ... per portion 6d.
Cigarettes & Chocolate
Spirits : Beers : Minerals, etc.
(As available)

Children under three years of age, free ; three years & under 14 years, half-fares.

**TICKETS CAN BE OBTAINED IN ADVANCE
FROM THE STATIONS AND ACCREDITED RAIL TICKET AGENCIES**

Further information will be supplied on application to the stations, agencies, or to S. Cott District Passenger Manager, British Railways—Newcastle, Tel. 2-0741.

CONDITIONS OF ISSUE

These tickets are issued subject to the British Transport Commission's published Regulations and Conditions applicable to British Railways exhibited at their Stations or obtainable free of charge at station booking offices.

Luggage allowances are as set out in the conditions.

Published by British Railways (N.E. Region)—6/57   Printed in Great Britain.   T.P.W. Ltd. N/cle. CS
PLEASE TURN OVER

A ramblers' excursion ran from Newcastle to the Scottish Border country on 21 July – 10/9d return from Newcastle to Hawick, with tea at 6d per cup and a tongue sandwich for 11d.

existing BOAC building. This was the cheapest alternative, but the site offered no scope for expansion. This would be a major problem if 'twin unit' (i.e. eight coach) trains ever had to be accommodated.

2) A medium level station situated south of Ebury Bridge. This station could be built to allow for future extension to accommodate eight-coach trains. The major disadvantage of this scheme was that the station would be inconveniently situated for the BOAC terminal, and would therefore require a 'trav-o-lator' (as it was described) to connect the station to the BOAC terminal building.

3) A high level station by which the approaches would cross Ebury Bridge above road level. The station, which would be adjacent to the BOAC

One of only five of its type built, 59-seat Wickham motor brake second E50415 on exhibition at Battersea on 30 June 1957.
PHOTOGRAPH: HUGH DAVIES COLLECTION

building, would be built initially for four-coach trains but could be extended, if required, for eight-coach trains. Although this was the most expensive of the three schemes, it was considered to offer the best long-term option.

It was proposed to provide two additional tracks between Victoria and Feltham, with flyovers at Chiswick and Hounslow. The new line between Feltham and Heathrow would cross existing open space to near the boundary of the airport, and then proceed in a tunnel to a point within the central area of the airport. For reasons of economy, the tunnel was to be built on the 'cut and cover' method. It was suggested that further investigation be undertaken into long-term traffic development which might include an above-ground bulk fuel siding and depot near the perimeter of the airport, a below-ground extension of the railway to the air cargo and freight depot, a small goods station, and an additional passenger station at No.1 maintenance area (presumably for airport staff).

The cost of the new railway, including rolling stock, was estimated to be £15,465,000. Optional extras

Staple traffic – a westbound train of milk empties near Savernake, 17 August 1957. The locomotive is 2-8-0 No.4701; the 47XXs, incidentally, were one of the last two pre-Grouping GWR classes to remain intact. PHOTOGRAPH: IVO PETERS

were a second track over Grosvenor Bridge to ease the movement of traffic (£500,000) and additional platforms at Hounslow station so as to provide interchange facilities (£150,000). The operating costs of the proposed railway, including renewal and interest on capital, were estimated to be £1,050,000 per annum. It was calculated that, if the scheme were put in hand straight away – subject, of

course, to Parliamentary approval – the railway could be completed by 1963 and could be operating at a profit by 1964.

But, as the history books show, this well researched and well considered proposal did not become reality. Instead, it became one of life's 'might have beens' – albeit a rather intriguing one.

In 1957, British industry was still heavily dependent on coal. The country's first atomic power station had been opened only the previous year, and natural gas was still some twenty years into the future – in 1957, though, the essential fuel for industry was transported by the train-load. On 26 June 1957, J37 No.64598 passes Dundee Tay Bridge shed with a northbound train of coal wagons, some of which are wooden-bodied. PHOTOGRAPH: BRIAN MORRISON

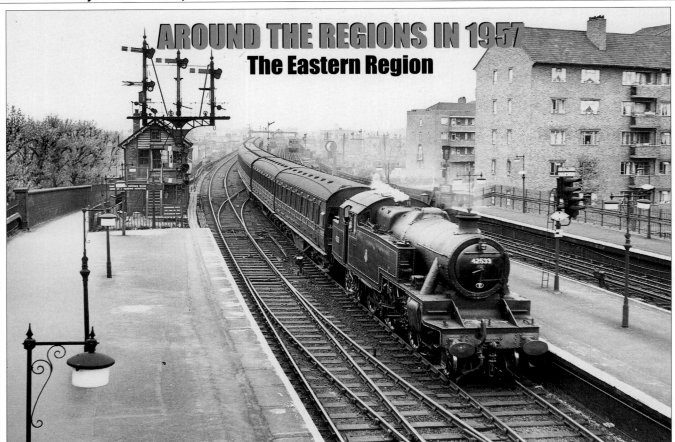

AROUND THE REGIONS IN 1957
The Eastern Region

The LT&S's epithet of the 'misery line' is not exclusive to recent times. In the 1950s, the line was plagued by staff shortages and, most usually, clapped out stock, but given that North Thameside was something of a boom area at the time, the train services were woefully inadequate. That said, over the years there *had* been attempts to update the stock – in the 1930s, for example, came the Stanier three-cylinder versions of the Fowler 2-6-4Ts. All 37 of these – Nos.42500-42536 – were still allocated to the LT&S line in the mid-1950s; on 4 May 1957 No.42533 of Plaistow shed brings a Southend-bound train into Bromley-by-Bow. PHOTOGRAPH: BRIAN MORRISON

Peppercorn A1 Pacific No.60139 coasts through Doncaster on 11 April 1957. PHOTOGRAPH: B.P.HOPER COLLECTION

You'll Remember those Black and White Days...

Heading a line of engines awaiting their turn to enter the New Works at Stratford on 31 August 1957 is D16/3 4-4-0 No.62576. The other types include a Sandringham 4-6-0, a WD 2-8-0 and a J17 0-6-0. Although locomotive construction had ceased at Stratford in 1924, the works continued to repair and overhaul locomotives for the best part of forty years; around the time our photograph was taken in 1957, the locomotives undergoing heavy overhauls at Stratford included two B1s, one B2, a B12, three J17s, two J20s, one J39, one J68, two J69s, one N2, one N7, an LMS Ivatt Class 4 2-6-0, a BR Standard Class 4 2-6-4T and three diesel shunters. PHOTOGRAPH: BRIAN MORRISON

Work-stained A1 Pacific No.60141 ABBOTSFORD pulls away from Kings Cross with an unidentified Pullman on 18 May 1957. PHOTOGRAPH: B.ROBERTSON; B.P.HOPER COLLECTION

An independent spirit

Even in 1957, the Easingwold Railway was an anachronism, albeit – for those who had a penchant for 'furry' rural railways – a delightful one. The Easingwold was an independent concern, unaffected by either the Grouping in 1922 or Nationalisation in 1948, but since its one and only locomotive had been condemned in 1947, it had hired a J71 or J72 from the LNER (and subsequently BR). Here, J71 No.68294 stands at Easingwold station with the company's ex-NER four-wheel brake composite. Apparently, throughout the whole of 1947 just one passenger had availed himself of the first class facility – this had accounted for the odd 8d (3½d) in the company's annual passenger receipts of £18.0s.8d. PHOTOGRAPH: NEVILLE STEAD COLLECTION

Even as late as 1957, not every railway which carried public traffic was state owned. The days of independent light railways – epitomised, perhaps, by the late Colonel Holman Fred Stephens – might have long since passed, but the 'Colonel Stephens' spirit lingered on, ironically, though, in the guise of two railways which had *not* been part of his empire. One was the Derwent Valley Light Railway and the other was the Easingwold Railway. The latter, however, closed its doors for the last time in 1957.

The Easingwold Railway had provided a connection between Alne, on the York-Northallerton main line, and the elegant market town of Easingwold for over 66 years, but it closed its metaphorical doors for the last time on 27 December 1957. For just over nine years it had been a goods only line, passenger services having been withdrawn on 29 November 1948. The Easingwold's main claim to fame was that it had spent its entire life as an independent concern, and by 1957 it was one of only two independent locomotive-worked public railways in Britain (other than preserved or pleasure railways) which were still operational.

The Easingwold Railway – all 2m 29ch of it – had opened to the public on 27 July 1891, an earlier opening date having had to be postponed following an unfavourable report from the Board of Trade. The BoT inspector, Major-General Hutchinson, had noted various requirements including: *'...some bushes, which impede the view of both level crossing gates, should be cut down... all facing points should be provided with iron gauge ties... a check rail should be placed round the curve of 8 chains radius near the commencement of the line... the down end of Alne Station platform should end in a ramp and some fencing should be removed from the same end of the platform... at Easingwold Station, a clock visible from the platform, name board, W.C. and urinal have yet to be provided'.* In most cases, such requirements were considered relatively minor and the railway in question was usually 'passed' for opening subject to the improvements being made, but in the case of the Easingwold there was another matter which effectively ruled out permission to open. This concerned the locomotive. Major-General Hutchinson opined that: *'...the Engine which is to work the line has only four wheels, which description of Engine has for years past been considered unsuitable for drawing passenger trains...'.* The locomotive in question was a Hudswell Clarke 0-4-0ST, but following the Board of Trade's edict an 0-6-0ST was hastily ordered as a replacement.

As mentioned earlier, the Easingwold Railway retained its independent status until the end, having escaped, not only the grouping in 1923, but also Nationalisation in 1948. In 1948, the British Transport Commission reported on all the minor railways which had not been scheduled in the Transport Act of the previous year, and the pertinent details for the Easingwold Railway (for 1947) were given as follows:
Gross receipts: £2,802
Expenditure: £4,830
Net Receipts: £2,028 DR
Misc. Receipts: £190
Net Revenue: £1,838 DR
Stock owned: One steam locomotive (out of service and beyond reasonable repair); one brake composite carriage.
Recommendation: *'...the line should not be absorbed, but the results should be reviewed from time to time to see if the position has changed'.*

The Easingwold continued to avoid absorption by BR (or was it that BR wasn't too keen to inherit the loss-making concern?), and carried on as an independent. That said, it should be emphasised that the railway's on-going independent status should not be confused with total self-sufficiency.

You'll Remember those Black and White Days...

When it came to motive power, the Easingwold's own locomotve had been condemned in 1947 and since then the company had had to rely on a locomotive hired from the LNER (later BR). The usual steed was a J71 or J72 0-6-0T, and the last engine to work the line was J72 No.68698 which, at 2.45pm on 27 December 1957, left Easingwold for Alne with a train comprising a long wheelbase parcels van, two covered goods vans, three open wagons of sugar beet and an empty mineral wagon.

Easingwold station on a misty day. Scheduled passenger services had ceased in 1948; the vehicle seen behind the locomotive is parcels van E70221E, the company's only remaining item of rolling stock. PHOTOGRAPH: NEVILLE STEAD COLLECTION

It was inevitable that, prior to the complete closure of the Easingwold line in 1957, various societies quickly organised visits. One visit was by the Branch Line Society; the precise date is, unfortunately, unrecorded. PHOTOGRAPH: NEVILLE STEAD COLLECTION

One of the last regular steam hauled passenger services on the London Transport network ceased in November 1957. This was the shuttle service between Epping and Ongar – an enigmatic bastion of steam at the eastern end of the Central Line. The Epping branch had been opened by the GER in April 1865 and had passed to the LNER at the grouping in 1923. In the latter half of the 1930s the LNER, in conjunction with the London Passenger Transport Board, had started to electrify the line but, due largely to the hiatus of the war years, it was May 1947 before the Central Line 'tube' reached Leytonstone. The Central Line was extended to Epping on 25 September 1949, but that was as far as things got for another eight years.

The final part of the branch – the six-mile stretch between Epping and Ongar – was taken over by London Transport but continued to be worked by steam on a push-pull basis, usually with a former GER F5 2-4-2T or occasionally an N7 0-6-2T in charge. The designated engine was accommodated at the small shed at Epping, and a visitor on 23 July 1957 noted that the following Stratford

locomotives were outstationed there: F5s Nos.67193, 67200 and 67218, and J15s Nos.65440 and 65442. The J15s were used for the freight workings on the branch.

Despite the somewhat anachronistic nature of the push-pull workings, they operated fairly uneventfully. One conspicuous exception, though, was on 7 June 1957 when a fighter plane crashed near the line between Epping and North Weald, damaging the track. This caused the partial derailment of a branch train; although some of the carriages derailed, the locomotive – F5 No.67193 – and the rest of the train remained on the track. One of the branch's regular push-pull sets, incidentally, was formed by one ex-LNER and one former GCR carriage.

Somewhat inevitably, the plans to electrify the Epping-Ongar section were eventually dusted off. The date of 3 November 1957 was earmarked for the start of electric services, but that proved impracticable and the current was finally switched on at 1.30am on Friday 15 November 1957. The first regular Central Line trains operated on Monday 18th. The final steam workings on Saturday 16th were

handled by F5s Nos.67200, 67212 and 67218, but to the disappointment of steam enthusiasts, on the last day of steam a notice was displayed at Epping station prohibiting the taking of photographs.

Despite the extension of the electric services to Ongar, through trains did not actually operate beyond Epping. The power available from the existing electricity sub station at Epping was limited, and so the Epping-Ongar section had to be operated as a separate entity on a shuttle basis – similar, in fact, to how things had been in steam days. Indeed, the similarity was such that the service intervals of the old steam workings were perpetuated by the new electric trains. Futhermore, the Epping-Ongar section remained single track with just the one crossing place at North Weald. Despite the official changeover to electric services, for a while it was not unknown for steam traction to be used on an early morning Liverpool Street-Ongar train. Also, the goods services – principally coal to the station yards – remained steam hauled, usually by a J15, although diesel traction took over for the final period before the cessation of goods services in 1965.

Left. Until the electrification of the Epping-Ongar section in 1957, this was a common sight in peak hours at Ongar – a pair of F5 2-4-2Ts on the 'shuttle'. No.67200 with its wartime stovepipe chimney runs into the terminus at Ongar with its p&p set, using the 1949 loop to position itself behind the next departure, No.67213 waiting to depart for Epping with the next train. The signal box survived the electrification, although new colour light signalling replaced the old semaphores, while Ongar 'box and its counterpart at North Weald were equipped with new illuminated displays.

As an aside, the electrification of the Epping-Ongar section in 1957 prompted speculation that the redundant push-pull sets would be transferred to the Chesham branch. However, it was decided that the six ancient flat-roofed auto coaches in use on the latter were, despite the earliest dating back to 1898, in better condition that the more youthful Epping-Ongar sets, and so the transfer was not undertaken. Coincidentally, in December 1957 one of the Chesham shuttle sets was repainted in the standard mid-brown – its first repaint since 1950.

Snow on the line

In January 1957 London Transport introduced its prototype sleet tender, numbered ST1, for the purpose of de-icing conductor rails. The tender was constructed at Acton Works, and was intended to supersede the sleet locomotives, of which the out-of-date traction control equipment would be costly to replace. The intention was for two sleet tenders to be attached to an empty service train – one at the front and the other at the rear.

The tender was of a restricted height so as to give an unimpared view from the train driver's cab. It consisted of a specially constructed four-wheel bogie, to which was fitted de-icing equipment comprising three sets of crushing rollers, steel brushes, and de-icing sprays. One of the three sets of equipment dealt with the central negative rail, and the other two with the positive rail, according to which side of the track it was on. The tender was fitted with a small roller which rode on the positive rail, and when the roller dropped below a pre-determined level (at the rail-end ramps), a cut-off valve was activated and, if appropriate, the equipment on the opposite side of the tender came into action. Consequently, by this method it did not matter which side the positive rail was on as the tender adjusted automatically.

The rollers and brushes were lowered by compressed air, supplied by the train. The sprays were fed by an axle-driven pump from two interconnected 75- gallon tanks mounted on top of the bogie frame; delivery was at the rate of 0.9 gallons of de-icing fluid per mile. The pump could be cut out as required by disengaging a lever-operated dog clutch. To avoid damage to the pump in the event of all three sprays becoming blocked, the delivery pipe was fitted with a relief valve from which the fluid was returned to the tanks.

F5 No.67218 with its two-coach set at Ongar. Although Ongar was a terminus, it had been laid out a through station; the site on the extreme left was once occupied by an engine shed; it is believed the building was demolished in the 1940s. PHOTOGRAPH: R.C.RILEY

London Transport's sleet tender, numbered ST1, entered service in January 1957. Its method of operation is described in the text.

Following initial trials on the Picadilly Line, both sleet tenders were subsequently based at Northfields. It is tempting to ask how they coped with the 'wrong type of snow', but we would not be so churlish....

Capital Panniers
In February 1957 London Transport acquired its second 0-6-0PT from the Western Region. This was ex-WR No.5752, which became LT No.L91. It followed on the heels of No.7711, which in October 1956 had become LT No.L90. The two pannier tanks were purchased to replace ex-Metropolitan 'F' class 0-6-2Ts Nos.L49 and L51 which were, by then, well over half a century old and were in need of extensive refits. Both 0-6-2Ts were withdrawn early in 1957, but it was September before L49 was cut up at Neasden.

When LT had originally looked at replacing the 0-6-2Ts it had considered the options of diesel locomotives, but in view of the small number of hours which the locomotives were required to work, the outlay on diesels had been considered unjustifiable. The 0-6-0PTs suited LT's requirements admirably, although the first two examples, L90 and L91, weren't in the best of mechanical condition and had to be replaced (by two other 0-6-0PTs) in 1960/61. Between 1956 and 1963 a total of thirteen different 0-6-0PTs were purchased by LT, and the last two remained active until June 1971 – almost three years after the demise of steam on BR. *(A slightly lengthier look at 'Capital Panniers' appeared in RAILWAY BYLINES 1:3. You would have seen that, wouldn't you? – Ed)*

An antiquity
On 19 January 1957 an informal ceremony was held at Neasden Depot to mark the handing over to London Transport of a veteran locomotive for preservation. The locomotive was a single cylinder, chain driven, tramway type 0-4-0 which had been built by Messrs Aveling & Porter (W/No.807); between 1872 and 1894 it had worked on the Wotton Tramway (Quainton Road-Brill), a line which ultimately finished up as part of the London Transport empire and was steam worked until closure in 1935. This engine was one of a pair of Aveling & Porters which had been used on the Wotton Tramway; both had been sold in 1894 to Nether Heyford brickworks, near Weedon in Northants, but the other example, W/No.846, was subsequently cannibalised to provide spares for W/No.807. The brickworks closed in 1940, and ten years later W/No.807 was rescued by the Industrial Locomotive Society who, in conjunction with London Transport, restored it, as far as was practicable, to its original condition.

Top left. F5 2-4-2T No.67200 at Ongar, 6 October 1957. A new loop put in in 1949 had enabled an upgrading of the service, in lieu of electrification. At one time the power was to have come through to the terminus, though when this was cut back to Epping for cost reasons it did not stop the work extending to Blake Hall by accident! The new layout at Ongar allowed two 'shuttles' into the terminus at once at the peak hours. The arrival (see 67200 on page 48-49) would run in behind the train waiting to go out at the platform end (as 67200 here), drawing forward when the preceding train had left for Epping, to take up the same position. PHOTOGRAPH: A.E. BENNETT

Right. In 1956, London Transport purchased WR 0-6-0PT No.7711 as a replacement for one of its F class 0-6-2Ts. The 'matchbox', although not in perfect mechanical condition, suited LT very well, and so a second – No.5752 – was purchased in February 1957. The trendsetter, No.7711, was numbered L90 in LT stock; it was photographed at Neasden on 1 June 1957 in the company of 0-4-4T L44 which is now preserved at Quainton Road. PHOTOGRAPH: R.C.RILEY

AROUND THE REGIONS IN 1957
The North Eastern Region

On 13 May 1957, B16 4-6-0 No.61422 heads an up freight conveying scrap iron through Pontefract (Baghill). Of the seventy B16s which had been built between 1919 and 1924, LNER No.925 had been damaged beyond repair during the air raid on York in 1942 but, otherwise, the class survived intact until the end of 1957 – the first 'ordinary' withdrawal took place in January 1958. During 1957 the B16s were concentrated mainly at York, Neville Hill and Heaton sheds, with isolated representatives at Selby and Starbeck. They were mixed traffic engines, and their regular passenger outings included the Newcastle-Carlisle and the York-Scarborough lines; their goods duties were varied, but there was an unusual foray in September 1957 when No.61430 (of York shed) had a spell working heavy mineral trains beteeen Blaydon and Consett. PHOTOGRAPH: P.COOKSON; NEVILLE STEAD COLLECTION

Throughout the 1950s, the J27 0-6-0s continued to perform excellent work in the north-east, although many of the class were by then around fifty years old. Indeed, some of the class survived to see their sixtieth birthdays in the mid-1960s. Several of the class were allocated to Sunderland shed, and although used principally on coal traffic, were certainly no strangers to general goods work. Here, No.65893 approaches South Pelaw Junction near Chester-le-Street while *en route* from Sunderland to Stella Gill Yard on 20 April 1957. PHOTOGRAPH: G.M.STADDON; NEVILLE STEAD COLLECTION

Heaton shed's A3 Pacific No.60072 SUNSTAR is in immaculate condition at Newcastle on 19 September 1957. PHOTOGRAPH: J.ROBERTSON; B.P.HOPER COLLECTION

The A8 class 4-6-2Ts were rebuilds of ex-NER 4-4-4Ts, all forty-five locomotives having been dealt with between 1931 and 1936. The year 1957 saw the first withdrawal of A8s, a consequence of the increasing use of DMUs in the north-east. However, the locomotive seen here, No.69857, was not actually withdrawn until February 1960; it was photographed on 20 April 1957 arriving at Durham with a train from Sunderland to Middleton-in-Teesdale. Three A8s were actually allocated to Durham shed – a sub of Sunderland (54A) – from Autumn 1957; two of those remained until the shed closed in 1960. PHOTOGRAPH: P.B.BOOTH; NEVILLE STEAD COLLECTION

Casings and chimneys

The first Bulleid lightweight Pacific to be rebuilt was No.34005 BARNSTAPLE, which was dealt with in May/June 1957. In its unrebuilt guise – a few months earlier, on 8 September 1956 – the locomotive stands amid heaps of discarded firebox remains at Nine Elms. PHOTOGRAPH: BRIAN MORRISON

Throughout railway history, locomotive engineers have constantly striven to improve the performance and efficiency of their machines. Occasionally, engineers didn't get things quite right first time, and what seemed like an excellent idea on the drawing board proved to be a little disappointing in practice. In some cases it was necessary to undertake fairly extensive rebuilding of the errant steeds, but in most cases relatively minor modifications – often stemming from newly-developed ideas – did the trick. During the course of 1957, some very high-profile locomotive classes underwent certain changes; these ranged from the extensive to the subtle.

The Bulleid Pacifics

One of the biggest alterations made to any type of locomotives during the 1950s was the rebuilding of the SR's Bulleid Pacifics. The first of Oliver Bulleid's two Pacific classes to appear were the Merchant Navys, which encountered widespread controversy from the very moment the class leader – No.21C1 (named CHANNEL PACKET, and eventually renumbered 35001) - left the erecting shop at Eastleigh on 17 February 1941. The main reasons for the controversy were that the locomotive not only bristled with innovative design features, but also that it was swathed in 'air-smoothed' casing; many observers described the locomotive's outer casing as 'streamlining', but Bullied positively loathed that word. An altogether less flattering alternative was the class's

nickname of 'Spamcans'; it is reputed that Bulleid actually banned the use of that nickname at Eastleigh! Cosmetically, with the new Pacific it was a case of 'love it or loathe it'. Indifference was not an option.

The locomotive's critics (of which there were many) were quick to point out that, despite the need for strict economies during the war years, the construction of No.21C1 had gone almost 50% over budget – the original estimated cost had been £16,000, but the final bill was £23,840. Furthermore, the Civil Engineer's original caution turned to near apoplexy when it was discovered that the locomotive's actual weight was over 99½ tons – i.e. seven tons more than the original estimated weight.

Among the new design features was a three-throw crank shaft, chain driven from the driving axle, which operated the valve gear for each of the three cylinders. The whole of the valve motion, crank axle and connecting rod were enclosed in an oil bath, the theory being that these parts would need no attention during the entire period between one works overhaul and the next. The practice, however, was somewhat different. It was soon found that the valve motion lost its adjustment very quickly, and the 'all enclosed' set-up was actually a hindrance to simple maintenance. This was just one of many grumbles which the new Pacifics generated, although to redress the balance, the men who had to work with the locomotives day in and day out had nothing but praise for the design of boiler.

The controversy surrounding the Merchant Navy Pacifics was still in full swing when, in September 1944, an order was placed for the construction of lightweight versions of the locomotives. These were the West Country class engines, intended initially for the Southern Railway's 'withered arm' (west of Exeter) and the Eastern Section business trains. The West Country versions (and their offshoots, the Battle of Britain class) incorporated all the principal Merchant Navy features including, ominously, the troublesome oil bath. The boilers of the West Country Pacifics were of a similar design to those fitted to the Merchant Navys – albeit with reduced firebox and grate areas – and this prompted the criticism that the engines would have power capabilities far beyond the requirements of their intended everyday duties. Or, as it was sometimes put, they were 'Rolls Royces doing Ford jobs'. In certain quarters this was considered to be yet another distasteful extravagance.

The non-conformity of the Bulleid Pacifics – Merchant Navys, West Countries and Battle of Britains – gave them a high public profile and, although many of the comments were far from favourable, it could not be denied that, particularly in the austerity conditions during and immediately after the war, the locomotives provided the Southern Railway with considerable publicity. There was, however a pay-back. The Pacifics proved costly to run and maintain; in the case of the Merchant

Navy Pacifics, in the mid-1950s their average coal consumption was stated to be 50.6lb per train mile compared to 43.9lb of LM Duchesses and 42.3lb of BR Britannias, while their repair costs per mile were 5.98p compared to 5.29p (Duchesses) and 3.66p (Britannias).

This resulted in the decision, in 1955, to rebuild Merchant Navy No.35018 BRITISH INDIA LINE as a far more conventional machine. The rebuilding involved dispensing with the oil bath and replacing the original inside cylinder and valve arrangement with a set-up incorporating three independent sets of Walschaert's valve gear. Also, the sometimes unpopular steam reversing gear was replaced by a screw gear, and the fabricated smokebox was replaced by one of orthodox cylindrical shape. Cosmetically, the biggest change was the removal of the air-smoothed casing. The boiler – the undisputed strongpoint of the original design – remained unaltered (save for a new type of superheater with a reduced heating surface), but to bring it up to contemporary specifications a rocking grate of the standard BR type and an entirely new ashpan were fitted.

The rebuilding work was completed in February 1956, and five other Merchant Navys were similarly treated before the year was out. Even before the work on No.35018 was finished, fifteen lightweight Pacifics were earmarked for rebuilding. Work started on the first of these – No.34005 BARNSTAPLE – in May 1957; the task was completed some six weeks later,

the engine leaving the erecting shop at Eastleigh on 26 June.

The rebuilding of No.34005 in 1957 was along very similar lines to that of the Merchant Navys – three independent sets of Walschaert's valve gear, removal of the oil bath, new smokebox, removal of the air-smoothed casing etc etc. Also, its cab was increased to 9ft width; the first seventy lightweight Pacifics (among them No.34005) had originally been built with cabs which were only 8ft 6in wide in order to fit the Hastings line gauge, but the introduction of diesel-electric services on the Hastings line in 1957 meant that the Pacifics would not be required there. The total cost of rebuilding No.34005 was a whopping £11,472.

After re-entering traffic, No.34005's first passenger duty was on 4 July 1957 when Eastleigh used it to work the 11.28am Eastleigh-Bournemouth Central, returning with the 4.34pm Bournemouth Central-Eastleigh. Those turns were actually part of Nine Elms duty No.72. On 5 and 6 July, and for most of the week ending 13 July, the engine was used on Eastleigh duty No.272, which comprised mainly cross country working over the Netley line, with a trip to Reading with the 5.16pm ex-Portsmouth. During late July No.34005 was usually to be found on Eastleigh express duties Nos.252 and 253, although on 3 August it hauled the 11.40am Weymouth-Bedford holiday special as far as Brent. A few days later the engine was transferred to Stewarts Lane, from where it was

put to work on the Victoria-Dover/Folkestone boat trains. It performed commendably. The next fourteen rebuilds were also allotted to the Eastern Section, but most of their work was on the business trains. Many later rebuilds were dispatched – or, to be precise, returned – to the Western Section, but this was not without its problems on the 'withered arm'. The rebuilding increased the engines' axleweights from 18tons 15cwt to 20tons 18cwt, and so they were prohibited from the North Devon, Cornwall and Plymouth lines. The prohibition from the Plymouth line was lifted in 1960, but remained on the two other routes.

The official party line was that the rebuilding of the two types of Bulleid Pacifics was a major improvement and enabled the locomotives' true potential to be realised. This view seemed to go publicly unchallenged for a while, but before too long there were stirrings from the 'anti-rebuilding' lobby who proclaimed that the Pacifics had been very good locomotives indeed before rebuilding, and that the rebuilding had actually been a retrograde step. In 1966 a total of 150 Western Section drivers who had worked with the engines before and after rebuilding were asked to sign a testimonial that the unrebuilt versions were better performers and ran more freely and, of those drivers, 80 – i.e. just over half – agreed with the sentiment and signed accordingly. Unfortunately, we are not informed whether the other seventy drivers disagreed with the sentiment, or were merely indifferent.

No.34017 ILFRACOMBE was one of the Bulleid lightweight Pacifics to be rebuilt in 1957. It emerged from the works in its new guise in November. It was photographed at Ramsgate in August the following year. PHOTOGRAPH: W.HERMISTON; B.P.HOPER COLLECTION

After experiments with No.7018 in 1956, No.4090 DORCHESTER CASTLE was fitted with a double chimney in 1957. On 20 April – soon after returning to service – it was photographed on Hatton Bank with the down Cambrian Coast Express. PHOTOGRAPH: R.C.RILEY

On the whole, it is somewhat conspicuous that today's 'anti-rebuilding' faction comprises mainly ex-railwaymen or amateur enthusiasts who had contacts in the running department, while those who side with the 'pro-rebuilding' lobby usually point to the pounds, shillings and pence. It has sometimes been suggested that the financial benefits of rebuilding were exaggerated by BR's accountants in order to overcome any opposition but, not altogether surprisingly, alternative sets of figures have never come to light. Unfortunately, it is rather unlikely that we shall ever know whether the financial statistics supporting the case for rebuilding were wholly reliable.

These days, the rebuilding of the Bulleid Pacifics generates considerable controversy in the pages of the railway press – almost as much controversy, in fact, as when the locomotives first appeared in 1941. We are tempted to suggest that, had Oliver Bulleid been with us, he might have enjoyed a wry smile at the thought that his locomotives still prompt heated debate in the late 1990s! We do not intend to participate in the debate at this point; we sit firmly astride the fence and merely present some of the 'pros' and 'cons'.

Returning to the year of 1957, the lightweight Pacifics rebuilt were as follows:

34001 EXETER - ex-works 11/57
34003 PLYMOUTH - ex-works 9/57

34005 BARNSTAPLE - ex-works 6/57
34013 OKEHAMPTON - ex-works 10/57
34017 ILFRACOMBE - ex-works 11/57
34022 EXMOOR - ex-works 12/57
34025 WHIMPLE - ex-works 11/57
34027 TAW VALLEY - ex-works 9/57

At the end of 1957, No.34022 was allocated to Ramsgate and all the others to Bricklayers Arms.

Also during 1957, the programme of rebuilding the Merchant Navys continued. The locomotives dealt with during the year were:

35008 ORIENT LINE - ex-works 5/57
35009 SHAW SAVILL - ex-works 3/57
35010 BLUE STAR - ex-works 1/57
35012 UNITED STATES LINES - ex-works 2/57
35016 ELDERS FYFFES - ex-works 4/57
35017 BELGIAN MARINE - ex-works 3/57
35023 HOLLAND AFRIKA LINE - ex-works 2/57
35026 LAMPORT & HOLT LINE - ex-works 1/57
35027 PORT LINE - ex-works 5/57

Double chimneys
One of the most famous achievements in railway history is that of LNER A4 Pacific No.4468 MALLARD which, on 3 July 1938, achieved a speed of 126mph near Essendine, on the East Coast Main Line between Grantham and Peterborough. The figure which entered the record books was actually 125mph, but even without the extra one mile per hour, it still stands as the world record for a steam locomotive. It is hardly likely to be beaten in the future.

One of the reasons why MALLARD had been selected for the world record run was that it had been built with a double blastpipe and chimney, which significantly improved the locomotive's draughting. The double chimney arrangement had first been seen on the LNER in May 1934 when P2 2-8-2 No.2001 COCK O'THE NORTH entered service; double chimneys had subsequently been used on W1 4-6-4 No.10000 and A3 4-6-2 No.2751 HUMORIST. The last three A4 Pacifics – Nos.4901, 4902 and 4903, completed in June and July 1938 – were also built with double blastpipes and chimneys. The advantages of this arrangement were already widely appreciated, but it was considered that the equipment would interfere with routine tube cleaning and so the other A4s were not similarly converted. At least, not just yet...

Things changed in 1957. In the preceding years some of the A4s had experienced steaming problems, especially with inferior coal, and it was eventually considered that the fitting of double blastpipes and chimneys would alleviate the problem. Starting in May 1957, the remaining thirty-one A4s were thus fitted; the programme was completed in November 1958. The A4s dealt with in 1957 were:

60002 SIR MURROUGH WILSON- ex-works 7/57
60003 ANDREW K.McCOSH - ex-works 7/57
60004 WILLIAM WHITELAW - ex-works 12/57
60006 SIR RALPH WEDGWOOD - ex-works 9/57
60007 SIR NIGEL GRESLEY - ex-works 12/57
60010 DOMINION OF CANADA - ex-works 12/57
60014 SILVER LINK - ex-works 10/57

60015 QUICKSILVER - ex-works 8/57
60016 SILVER KING - ex-works 6/57
60017 SILVER FOX - ex-works 5/57
60018 SPARROW HAWK - ex-works 10/57
60019 BITTERN - ex-works 9/57
60020 GUILLEMOT - ex-works 11/57
60026 MILES BEEVOR - ex-works 8/57
60028 WALTER K.WIGHAM - ex-works 11/57

On the Western Region, Swindon Works continued to equip its front-line motive power with twin blastpipes and double chimneys during 1957. This was part of an on-going programme which had been instigated in 1955 when King class 4-6-0 No.6015 KING RICHARD III had been experimentally fitted with a double chimney. In subsequent tests with ordinary service trains, No.6015 had comfortably exceeded 100mph on a number of occasions. On one occasion a speed of over 107mph had been recorded and, although GWR partisans weren't averse to 'inflating' performance figures, it is now generally accepted that 107mph was indeed exceeded. This is the highest speed ever attributed to an ex-GWR locomotive.

Following the transformation of No.6015, it was decided to equip the remainder of the Kings with double chimneys. One of the class was dealt with in December 1955, fourteen in 1956, ten in 1957, and the other four in 1958. The first twelve originally received narrow fabricated chimneys (as had been fitted to No.6015), but from November 1956 a more pleasing cast iron chimney of elliptical cross-section was used. Those engines with fabricated chimneys were later refitted

with cast iron chimneys. For the record, the Kings dealt with in 1957 were as follows (mileages to date shown in brackets):

6003 KING GEORGE IV - ex-works 4/57 (1,673,746)
6008 KING JAMES II - ex-works 7/57 (1,405,184)
6014 KING HENRY VII - ex-works 9/57 (1,607,661)
6019 KING HENRY V - ex-works 4/57 (1,643,648)
6021 KING RICHARD II - ex-works 3/57 (1,490,006)
6023 KING EDWARD II - ex-works 6/57 (1,315,191)
6024 KING EDWARD I - ex-works 3/57 (1,320,206)
6025 KING HENRY III - ex-works 3/57 (1,549,030)
6028 KING GEORGE VI - ex-works 1/57 (1,388,243)
6029 KING EDWARD VIII - ex-works 12/57 (1,624,250)

The fitting of double chimneys to the Kings was considered successful, and so it was not altogether surprising that the Castle class 4-6-0s were similarly treated. The first Castle to be dealt with was No.7018 in May 1956; as with the Kings, the first conversions incorporated fabricated chimneys but later conversions (starting in April 1957) had elliptical copper-capped chimneys. The fitting of double chimneys to the Castles was a comparatively protracted affair, and by the end of 1961 – when the programme ceased – only 66 of the 152 survivors had been dealt with. During 1957, only two Castles were dealt with:

4090 DORCHESTER CASTLE - ex-works 4/57 (1,578,437)
4093 DUNSTER CASTLE - ex-works 12/57 (1,612,888)

It should not go unremarked that No.4093 spent 308 days at Swindon in 1957 – it was booked into the works on 16 March and was ex-works on 10 December.

The WR's enthusiasm for double chimneys extended to the County class 4-6-0s. Ironically, perhaps, the first of the class, No.1000, had been fitted with a double chimney from new, but the chimney was poorly proportioned and actually had a detrimental effect on the locomotive's performance. Following trials with alternative types of double chimneys in the mid-1950s, the whole class was eventually fitted wirth cast iron copper-cap double chimneys; these were similar to, but considerably shorter than, those fitted to the Kings. Eight of the Counties were dealt with in 1957 (mileages in brackets):

1001 COUNTY OF BUCKS - ex-works 12/57 (503,740)
1003 COUNTY OF WILTS - ex-works 11/57 (510,872)
1004 COUNTY OF SOMERSET - ex-works 4/57 (489,217)
1007 COUNTY OF BRECKNOCK - ex-works 5/57 (492,853)
1010 COUNTY OF CAERNARVON-ex-works 1/57 (523,891)
1012 COUNTY OF DENBIGH - ex-works 9/57 (608,742)
1016 COUNTY OF HANTS - ex-works 3/57 (426,656)
1023 COUNTY OF OXFORD - ex-works 5/57 (427,357)

A4 Pacific No.60018 SPARROW HAWK was ex-works with its double chimney in October 1957. It was photographed at Portobello West on 6 July the following year. PHOTOGRAPH: J.ROBERTSON; B.P.HOPER COLLECTION

AROUND THE REGIONS IN 1957
The Scottish Region

A2 Pacific No.60525 – named after its creator, A.H.PEPPERCORN – with empty stock at Haymarket on 26 May 1957. The cleanliness of the locomotive is a credit to the staff at the shed. PHOTOGRAPH: J.ROBERTSON; B.P.HOPER COLLECTION

The new breed at St.Margaret's... North British-built 200hp diesel shunter No.11704 stands on the turntable on 7 July 1957. Under the renumbering scheme of 1957, this locomotive became D2704. It survived in BR stock only until June 1967 when it was sold for scrap. It was less than twelve years old. So – these new-fangled dieasels were meant to be a long-term option, were they? PHOTOGRAPH: B.P.HOPER COLLECTION

You'll Remember those Black and White Days...

'Improved Director' D11 4-4-0 No.62690 THE LADY OF THE LAKE was one of twenty-four locomotives ordered by Nigel Gresley for the LNER to a design which had originated with John Robinson on the Great Central Railway in pre-Grouping days. The twenty-four LNER examples were intended for use on the North British section in Scotland, and after entering service were given names with a Walter Scott theme; 'Scott' names had previously been used by the North British for two classes of 4-4-0s (and also, it should be noted, by the staunchly English GWR for a batch of 4-6-0s and 4-4-2s which had been built in 1905). Several of the LNER's 'Scottish Directors' survived until 1961; one of those was No.62690, looking very smart at Edinburgh on 5 April 1957. One of the earlier GCR examples – BUTLER HENDERSON – is now preserved. PHOTOGRAPH: G.M.STADDON; NEVILLE STEAD COLLECTION

Framed by the impressive signal gantry at Greenock Princes Pier, the stock for a Glasgow St.Enoch train is being marshalled by Pickersgill 3P 4-4-0 No.54468 on 22 June 1957. This class of archetypal Caledonian engines remained intact until Spring 1959 although, as evidenced here, by the latter part of the 1950s their cosmetic condition could leave a little to be desired. During the mid- and late 1950s, the sixteen locomotives were widely dispersed in Scotland, being represented at ten different sheds – Inverness, Helmsdale, Forres, Perth, Forfar, Dalry Road, St.Rollox, Greenock, Motherwell, Hamilton. PHOTOGRAPH: BRIAN MORRISON

One of Britain's most fascinating standard gauge industrial railway systems was at Beckton gas works in East London. This was no ramshackle Mickey Mouse operation; in the mid-1950s the gas works had a stud of around forty steam locomotives and there was another dozen based at the adjacent by-products works. At the gas works themselves, there were no less than three engine sheds; one of these was a substantial roundhouse with a 20ft turntable and fifteen stabling roads, eight of which had pits. Many of the Beckton locomotives were real veterans, but they were invariably maintained in first-class condition; the gas works engines were painted apple green with red connecting rods, while the by-products works used a maroon livery. At the gas works, the locomotives had to negotiate restricted clearances and so most were cabless, while a handful which had to run through the severely limited openings of the retort houses were specially built to 'cut down' dimensions. One of the cabless locos was 0-4-0ST No.40, which had been built by the Hunslet Engine Co in 1919. It was photographed during a special visit on 24 August 1957. PHOTOGRAPH: R.C.RILEY

THE INDUSTRIAL SCENE IN 1957

There was – and, to an extent, still is – more to Britain's railways than main lines and branches. We're talking industrials – those intriguing little systems, often with archaic locomotives, ramshackle infrastructure, and working practices which seemed to owe more to the 'suck it and see' school of thought than to any rulebook. During the 1950s the interest in industrial railways was not particularly widespread. After all, there was oodles of steam activity in all sorts of guises on BR lines throughout Britain, and so a humble little Manning Wardle pug shunting a few coal wagons at a gas works siding was, in the eyes of most, not particularly interesting, not least of all because it couldn't be underlined in the ABC. To put it another way, industrial railways were the non-league faction while BR was Premier Division – some regarded supporting Enfield Town rather eccentric when, a few miles down the road, one could see Spurs or Arsenal. But while the industrial sector – and Enfield Town – might have lacked glamour, they had undisputed charisma.

Attitudes towards industrial railways changed in the 1960s. With the rapid run-down and abrupt extinction of BR steam during that decade, enthusiasts began to take notice of industrial sites where steam was still active. At some sites – particularly collieries, where there was a constant supply of locomotive fuel – steam engines remained in everyday use until the late 1970s (and a few lingered on into the 1980s), and this resulted in the attractions of industrial railways being brought home to a much wider audience. No longer were industrial enthusiasts regarded as 'non-leaguers', as had often been the case in the past. Although many industrial sites have now closed, and although those that survive have dispensed with steam locomotives, the interest in industrial railways these days is, perhaps, greater than ever. This has been due largely to the dedication of the Industrial Railway Society, the Industrial Locomotive Society and the Narrow Gauge Society, while in the commercial field, the popular Irwell Press magazine *Railway Bylines* includes regular coverage of industrial systems. The 'spreading of the word' is an on-going process...

Looking at 1957, there were some awesome industrial railway systems to be seen. To quote just three random examples... At the Royal Docks in London – just one of three dock systems operated by the Port of London Authority – the internal railway system comprised *seventy* miles of track and was worked by a fleet of twenty-three steam locomotives; the Skinningrove Ironworks at Carlin How in North Yorkshire has a stud of nineteen operational locos, while the charismatic 1ft 10¾in-gauge system serving Penrhyn Quarries in North Wales had twelve steam locomotives in stock for working at the quarry levels and also on the four-mile long 'main line' to Port Penrhyn.

Around the country, there was so much industrial activity to see, but comparatively few enthusiasts bothered to investigate until the latter part of the 1960s. Unfortunately, for reasons of space we can provide only a very brief glimpse here.

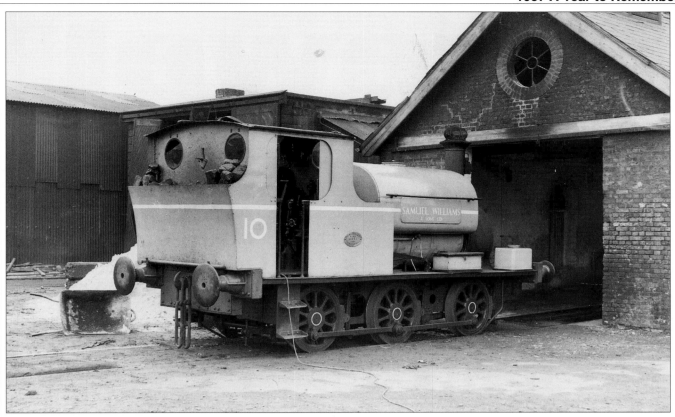

Another well-known standard gauge industrial system in the Greater London area was that of Messrs.Samuel Williams & Sons, the owners of Dagenham Dock. In 1955, the first of a series of 'Planet' diesel shunters was purchased, and just two years later, diesels completely ousted the stud of steam locomotives. Although Samuel Williams was constantly modernising its operations – as evidenced by the comparatively early switch from steam to diesel – some of its steam locomotives were real veterans. Among them was an 0-6-0ST which, it was later discovered, was Hunslet Engine Co Works No.1 of 1865 – i.e. the very first locomotive to have been constructed by this famous builder. Among the other Williams locomotives was No.10, a Hudswell Clarke 0-6-0ST of 1924, which had been purchased secondhand in 1940. It was the first Williams locomotive to be painted in the startling light blue livery; it is seen outside the engine shed at Dagenham Dock on 9 March 1957, its last year of operation. PHOTOGRAPH: R.C.RILEY

Who said that industrial railways were 'just a pug and a siding'? This intriguing view shows the Felin Fawr incline on the 1ft 10¾in-gauge Penrhyn Quarry system in June 1957. Ascending wagons are on the left; in the foreground, the flat-sided wagon was used to carry sacks of slate dust. PHOTOGRAPH: DEREK CLAYTON

Farewell

Not so much 'farewell', but more 'welcome back'... CITY OF TRURO being oiled at Swindon shed yard on 18 August 1957. (See pages 68/69). PHOTOGRAPH: BRIAN MORRISON

During the course of 1957, the withdrawal of various locomotives resulted in the total extinction of a handful of classes. Old ones, new(ish) ones, loved ones, neglected ones, as they used to say....

Highland Railway 0-4-4Ts

The first class to be rendered extinct in 1957 was the ex-Highland Railway 'Passenger Tank' 0-4-4Ts. The class had comprised only four locomotives,

which had been built at Lochgorm Works in 1905/06 to a Peter Drummond design. They were intended for lightly laid branch lines, in particular the Dornoch and the Wick & Lybster Light Railways which the HR worked. At the grouping the four became LMS Nos.15051-15053, and at the time of Nationalisation two were still active; these became BR Nos.55051 and 55053. By then, both were allocated to Helmsdale for

working the Dornoch branch, the usual practice being for one to be outstationed at Dornoch for a fortnight at a time. Of the two engines, No.55051 was withdrawn in July 1956, being in need of heavy repairs. This left No.55053, not only as the sole survivor of its class, but also as the last active Highland Railway locomotive of any description. Befitting its celebrity status, No.55053 sported a well maintained lined black livery; this had been applied at St.Rollox Works in July 1955, and was the only instance of the full BR passenger livery being applied to a former HR engine. No.55053 continued to work the Dornoch branch, and following the demise of its classmate it shared the duties with Caley 2P 0-4-4T No.55236 — a somewhat heavy beast for the line, despite the fact that the branch had had its axleweight limit raised from 12 to 14 tons.

The distinguished career of No.55053 came to an abrupt end on 16 November 1956. While on a routine branch working – one corridor coach and a couple of fish vans – the locomotive's leading coupled axle broke; one wheel parted company from the axle and ran along the ballast but, fortunately, the engine and train remained on the rails and nobody was hurt. The locomotive was taken to Lochgorm Works to await a decision as to its future. Not altogether surprisingly, replacement running gear was not readily available; with a

You'll Remember those Black and White Days...

After suffering a broken axle in November 1956, 0-4-4T No.55053 – the last ex-Highland Railway locomotive in ordinary service – was laid aside at Lochgorm Works at Inverness to await a decision as to its future. The decision was not long in coming; in January 1957 it was announced that the locomotive was to be withdrawn. No.55053 languished at Lochgorm for some time, and was not cut up until February 1958. It was photographed on 24 June 1957; as can be seen, apart from the wheels it was still intact. PHOTOGRAPH: BRIAN MORRISON

lack of foresight, when classmate No.55051 had been withdrawn earlier in 1956 it had been cut up within a matter of weeks, and so a potentially useful source of spares had been done away with. It was, therefore, impossible for No.55053 to be economically repaired. The only alternative was withdrawal, and this officially took place during the week ending 12 January 1957. It was, however, February 1958 before the locomotive was cut up.

On the Dornoch branch, the sudden incapacitation of No.55053 in November 1956 caused a problem. Due to the weight limit imposed on the branch the list of suitable locomotives was somewhat brief, and as a temporary – and not particularly ideal – measure a 2MT 2-6-0 was drafted in. However, a longer-term replacement was soon identified, and it came in an unexpected guise. It was Western Region 16XX class 0-6-0PT No.1646, which left its home of Croes Newydd on 7 February 1957 (being incorporated into a goods train) and arrived at Helmsdale four days later. No.1646 proved to be very well suited to the branch, and so, in 1958, classmate No.1649 was also despatched to Helmsdale for duties on the Dornoch branch.

The two pannier tanks retained their status as the regular Dornoch branch locomotives until June 1960, when the branch closed to all traffic. The transfer of Nos.1646 and 1649 to Scotland prompted the suggestion that, with other 16XXs allocated to sheds in Cornwall, this dispersal of a class was almost certainly a peacetime record.

GWR Dean Goods 0-6-0s
Two famous GWR classes became

extinct in 1957. The first was the celebrated Dean Goods 0-6-0s, of which 260 had been built at Swindon between 1883 and 1899. They were very simple and reliable locomotives, and were used throughout the GWR network. Furthermore, during both world wars many of the class were requisitioned for service abroad. By the beginning of 1948 there were just 54 left to be taken into BR stock; many were, by then, concentrated in the Oswestry Division as they could be used on a number of ex-Cambrian lines which were out of bounds to heavier tender engines. In 1952/53, however, the allocation of Standard Class 2 2-6-0s to the Oswestry Division displaced almost all of the remaining Dean Goods from their last stronghold, and after the summer of 1955 the only survivors were Nos.2516 and 2538, both of which were then 58 years old. No.2516 was withdrawn in May 1956 and was subsequently acquired for exhibition at Swindon Museum, but No.2538 remained active at Oswestry for another year. Until May 1956 No.2538 had undertaken some of the freight workings on the Kerry branch, but after the complete closure of the branch that month the engine was put to work mainly on Oswestry-Whitchurch or Oswestry-Gobowen freights. It was, incidentally, routinely fitted with a snow plough during the winter months – clearly, it was not expected to shirk winter duties simply because of its age. Withdrawal for No.2538 finally came on 15 May 1957, the engine being marked 'Condemned' and dispatched to Swindon five days later for cutting up. A visitor to Swindon Works on 16 June noted that No.2538's boiler had already been removed. It was an insultingly swift demise.

GWR Star 4-6-0s
The other famous GWR design to disappear in 1957 was the Star class 4-6-0s. At the beginning of 1957 only two of the 73-strong class were left in service - No.4056 PRINCESS MARGARET and No.4061 GLASTONBURY ABBEY – but on 11 March the number was reduced to just one when No.4061 was withdrawn. Since April 1951 No.4061 had been allocated to Stafford Road shed, and as late as April/May 1955 had undergone a 'heavy general' at Swindon. It had been taken into Swindon Factory Pool on 8 February 1957 and had entered the works on 12 February, but was never to return to traffic. No.4061 was unceremoniously cut up at Swindon during the week ending 18 May, having notched up a very respectable 1,550,800 miles during its 35-year life.

The withdrawal of No.4061 meant that No.4056 PRINCESS MARGARET was the only remaining representative of the Star class. No.4056 was a Bath Road engine – indeed, in 1957 it was still inscribed with the 'BRD' shed stencil (not to mention the buffer beam number) – and had lived in Bristol since its transfer from Taunton in June 1948. It had, incidentally, also been allocated to Bath Road from 1928 to 1933. By 1957, No.4056 was in very poor mechanical condition (its last 'general' had been in 1953, since when it had run 180,000 miles), but it was still regularly rostered for secondary passenger workings between Bristol and Paddington (often working home with the 2.35pm via Devizes) and also Bristol-Salisbury turns. By way of a change, on 7 September 1957 it was noted arriving at Paddington with the 12.30pm ex-Newquay, but it seems that this had not been an auspicious journey as an observer remarked that the repair card put in by the driver was 'the fullest one I had ever seen'. Clear evidence of No.4056's condition was seen two days later when, as a late replacement for a failed Castle on the 7.15pm Paddington-Bristol passenger train, it got no farther than Ealing before having to stop for a blow up. It was taken off at Southall. According to the engine's repair records, just a week later – on 16 September – it was detained at Landore; this was presumably due to yet another failure, confirmed, perhaps, by an unsubstantiated report of the engine having a damaged nearside cylinder. No.4056 was held at Landore until 27 September, when it was taken under the wing of Swindon Pool to await entry to the works. It entered the works on 1 October, and in view of its mechanical condition, it seemed a foregone conclusion that it would be condemned. Formal withdrawal took place on 28 October, and the engine was subsequently cut up at Swindon. During its 43-year life No.4056 had run

The last two ex-GWR Star class 4-6-0s were withdrawn in 1957. The first of the pair to go was No.4061 GLASTONBURY ABBEY, which made its very last journey to Swindon Works in February 1957. Some six months or so earlier – on 25 July 1956 – No.4061 had what was, by then, a rare outing on the 7.45am Leamington Spa-Birkenhead train; it was photographed leaving Birmingham Snow Hill. PHOTOGRAPH: MICHAEL MENSING

2,074,338 miles; this was the record for the class.

Taff Vale 'A' class 0-6-2Ts

Another loss during 1957 were the last remaining locomotives of the Taff Vale Railway. At the grouping the GWR had inherited no less than 274 locomotives from the TVR, and these included various classes of 0-6-2Ts – a type which, in several guises, was used to remarkably good effect in South Wales. Among the TVR 0-6-2T types was the A class which, after the grouping, had been fitted with taper boilers and generally been 'Swindonised'. Apart from one withdrawal in November 1952 the class had remained intact until 1953 when Standard Class 3 2-6-2Ts arrived in the Cardiff Valleys Division, principally to take over the passenger duties formerly worked by the As. This was the beginning of the end for, not only the ex-TVR engines, but also the other surviving constituent engines in the Division.

Perhaps surprisingly, in 1953 and 1954 only five of the TVR A class engines were disposed of, but in 1955 the real massacre commenced. Twelve of the class were withdrawn in that year, while no less than 25 were dispensed with in 1956, leaving just 14 in service at the start of 1957. By then, they were the only remaining TVR locomotives of any description. The final nail in the locomotives' metaphorical coffin was the transfer, in March 1957, of five 41XX 2-6-2Ts from Birkenhead to Cathays (88A), principally to take over the A class engines' remaining passenger duties. This brought about the withdrawal of five As, and with two having been withdrawn earlier in 1957, this left just seven. These seven survivors were Nos.304, 370, 373, 381, 383, 390 and 398, which were all transferred to Abercynon (88E) to see out their days

on freight and shunting work. The last passenger workings undertaken by an A class 0-6-2T took place on 5 June when, amid considerable publicity, No.373 was specially rostered for what was usually an Aberdare turn (the duty had been 'given' to Abercynon for the day). The itinerary was: 1.20pm Merthyr-Cardiff (Bute Road) via the old Taff Vale main line; 3.00pm Cardiff (Bute Road) to Quakers Yard (H.L.) via Ystrad Mynach; 4.35pm Quakers Yard (L.L.) to Merthyr; 6.25pm Merthyr-Pontypridd; 7.10pm Pontypridd-Treherbert; 9.00pm Treherbert-Pontypridd; light engine Pontypridd-to Abercynon shed.

The seven remaining members of the A class were withdrawn from service in August. Nos.304 and 383 were dispatched to Swindon on 12 August, with Nos.370 and 398 following on 13 August. Of the other three, No.381 left Abercynon on 22 August and Nos.373 and 390 on 24 August, but these three initially went only as far as Cardiff East Dock shed where they were formally condemned, and did not depart for Swindon until the first week of September. Of those last three, No.373 had completed a 21-hour turn of duty at 2.30am on 22 August – only hours before being officially condemned.

Of the other TV A class engines which had been around at the start of 1957, No.361 was involved in a minor mystery. A few months after its withdrawal in January, it was allegedly sighted being towed to Newton Abbot where, according to local rumour, its boiler was to be reused on 2-6-2T No.4547. The rumour was, of course, totally unfounded, as the boilers weren't interchangeable, but that still leaves the question as to what No.361 was doing in Devon. Clearly, it had not been sent from Swindon to Newton Abbot merely for cutting up as

the scrap would eventually have had to be returned to Swindon. Maybe No.361 was destined for use as a stationary boiler? Or perhaps the whole episode was the result of a local observer in Devon over-indulging on farm-brewed scrumpy? We shall probably never know.

Rhymney Railway 'R' class 0-6-2Ts

Although the last days of the Taff Vale A class 0-6-2Ts attracted considerable attention, the last constituent engines to work in the Cardiff Valleys Division were actually the Rhymney Railway R class, which outdid the TVR As by a little over a month. The Rhymney R class engines were also 0-6-2Ts, but unlike their TVR counterparts they escaped being 'Swindonised' and saw out their days largely in their original condition.

At the start of 1957 four of the R class remained - Nos.36, 38, 42 and 43, all allocated to Cardiff East Dock shed. Of those, No.43 was withdrawn in February 1957 and No.42 in September; the latter had been laid up at East Dock shed with a hot box since late August, and following its official withdrawal was dispatched to Swindon for cutting up on 16 September. The last two representatives – Nos.36 and 38 – remained active for a few weeks longer, both being observed at work on several occasions in late September and early October. It is believed that the last revenue-earning task of all was undertaken by No.38 which, on 5 October, took a train of empties (Duty D7) from Cardiff Docks to Bargoed Colliery. On 7 October, Nos.36 and 38 left Cardiff for the last time, bound for Swindon, but No.36 developed problems with its safety valves *en route* and had to wait overnight at Gloucester. Both engines were formally condemned at Swindon on 8 October, and were cut up within a matter of weeks. The departure of the last two Rhymney engines from Cardiff in October 1957 was something of a coincidence as, exactly one hundred years earlier, in October 1857, the Rhymney Railway's first two locomotives (Vulcan Foundry 0-6-0s) had been delivered to Cardiff.

As a snippet of interest, at the time Nos.36 and 38 met their demise, another ex-Rhymney R class 0-6-2T was still intact, except for its coupling rods, at Worcester. This was No.35 which, a couple of months after being withdrawn in November 1956, had been dispatched to Worcester Works for stationary boiler duties. It remained there until January 1958.

LBSC/SR N15X 4-6-0s
Throughout railway history many locomotives were rebuilt, but few types underwent such a cosmetic transformation as the seven LB&SC L class 4-6-4Ts which, in the mid-1930s, were rebuilt as 4-6-0 tender engines. By the mid-1930s the spread of electrification on the old LB&SC network (by then, the Central Section of the SR) had made the L class virtually redundant on their native territory, hence their rebuilding as 4-6-0s for duties on the Western Section; the conversion from tank to tender format was necessary as, in common with almost all LB&SC types, the L class had not been designed to carry large amounts of water. In their former guises only three of the class had carried names, but as 4-6-0s all seven became named. The names were:

No.	Name
2327	TREVITHICK
	(formerly CHARLES C.MACRAE)
2328	HACKWORTH
2329	STEPHENSON
	(retained same name)
2330	CUDWORTH
2331	BEATTIE
2332	STROUDLEY
2333	REMEMBRANCE
	(retained same name)

The rebuilds were designated N15X, but were invariably referred to as the Remembrance class. No.2333, incidentally, had been the very last locomotive built for the LB&SC.

At Nationalisation the N15Xs became BR Nos.32327-32333. Two were withdrawn in 1955 and four in 1956, leaving No.32331 BEATTIE as the sole survivor. From its home shed of Basingstoke, its regular duties included Portsmouth services (passenger and goods) and Waterloo slows. No.32331 was specially booked to haul a ramblers' special from London Bridge to Windsor & Eton Riverside on 23 June 1957, and worked an empty stock train up from Basingstoke on 21st so as to be ready for the special. As far as can be determined, the special was the engine's last revenue earning activity prior to withdrawal in July.

PD&SWJR 0-6-2T
According to an old adage, 'the longer the name the shorter the railway'. This was rather true in the case of the Plymouth, Devonport & South Western Junction Railway, which worked nothing more than the 9½-mile branch

from Bere Alston to Callington, astride the Devon/Cornwall border. That said, it should be pointed out that, although the PD&SWJR also owned the main line between Plymouth and Lydford (via Bere Alston), the company never actually worked that section – working of the main line section was undertaken, initially, by the L&SWR and, later, the SR.

The Callington branch was a revised and extended version of an old narrow gauge mineral railway, the 'upgraded' line – a conventional standard gauge passenger carrying railway – being opened in 1908. For working the branch, the PD&SWJ purchased three new locomotives from Messrs Hawthorn Leslie. These were an 0-6-0T (No.3, named A.S.HARRIS) and two 0-6-2Ts (No.4 EARL OF MOUNT EDGCUMBE and No.5 LORD ST.LEVAN) which, at the grouping, were taken into SR stock as Nos.756, 757 and 758 respectively. They all survived to become BR stock. The 0-6-0T was withdrawn in 1951 without having had its allotted BR number (30756) applied. but the two 0-6-2Ts duly had their BR numbers (30757 and 30758) applied and held out for a few years. They remained allocated to Friary shed at Plymouth and had occcasional outings on Callington branch freights or shed pilot duties.

In mid-1956 the two 0-6-2Ts were dispatched to Eastleigh to work out their mileage. No.30758 LORD ST.LEVAN was in very poor condition and was soon retired, but No.30757 EARL OF MOUNT EDGCUMBE was

Withdrawal of the ex-Rhymney Railway R class 0-6-2Ts commenced in 1949, and the class became extinct in 1957, when the last four were condemned. The previous year, the on-going reduction had reduced the class total by three; one of those to go was No.44, seen here with a coal train at Pontypridd. PHOTOGRAPH: ALAN JARVIS

put to regular use, principally as shed and works pilot, but sometimes as station pilot. It was reported as being under repair at Eastleigh running shed in May 1957, but bearing in mind that the engine was 'completing its time' the repairs were presumably minor. No.30757 was withdrawn in December 1957; surprisingly, perhaps, the demise of the last of the PD&SWJR's three locomotives attracted negligible interest.

NER 'R' class (LNER D20) 4-4-0s
Depending on one's regional loyalties, it might be argued that the most distinguished class to become extinct in 1957 was the ex-NER 6ft 10in R class (later LNER D20 class) 4-4-0s. The class had originally comprised sixty engines, built at Gateshead Works to a Wilson Worsdell design between 1899 and 1907. In their heyday these graceful engines had worked the best NER expresses, but they were superseded by, firstly, 4-4-2s and, later, by 4-6-2s. Fifty of the sixty D20s were taken into BR stock; they were allotted numbers in the 62340-62397 series, but not all survived long enough to have their new numbers applied. By the mid-1950s the steadily dwindling band of survivors were concentrated mainly at Selby, Bridlington and Alnmouth. By the start of 1957 only seven remained.

The first D20 to go in 1957 was No.62397 of Bridlington, which was withdrawn in February. In May,

Nos.62375 and 62383 – both reported to be in very good external condition – were formally withdrawn from Alnmouth (sub to Tweedmouth, 53D), although No.62383 had actually departed for Darlington scrapyard on 26 April. No.62375, incidentally, was the last of the four class members which had been fitted with long travel valves - these four had been designated D20/2. To replace the withdrawn D20s at Alnmouth, Nos.62387 and 62395 were transferred from Bridlington and York respectively.

At Alnmouth, the D20s were used almost exclusively on the Alnwick-Newcastle trains. During the summer of 1957 a day's work for the one D20 in use normally involved taking out the 7.27am from Alnwick and returning with either the 12.27pm from Newcastle (SO) or the 5.04pm (SX). From mid-July to mid-August No.62395 was the only Almouth D20 in regular service, the other one, No.62387, having been sidelined at the parent shed at Tweedmouth awaiting repairs to a leaking tender. During No.62387's absence from Alnmouth, a V1 deputised.

Although No.62387 returned to duty at Alnmouth in mid-August 1957, it was withdrawn the following month. The other two surviving D20s – Nos.62381 and 62396 – were transferred to Alnmouth as replacements, where they joined No.62395, thereby concentrating the three remaining D20s at that shed.

However, that situation did not last for very long as all three were withdrawn in November and dispatched to Darlington for cutting up. It seems that two were cut up fairly promptly, as a visitor to Darlington on 12 January 1958 reported that only No.62395 was still intact. The report added that the engine had been repainted on one side, complete with the new BR crest, for an official photograph. Understandably, this raised hopes that the engine was destined for preservation, but that was not to be, and a month later all that remained of No.62395 were the wheels and the tender. It was an ignominious end.

GCR/LNER S1 0-8-4Ts
Four of these hefty shunting engines were built to a John Robinson design for the Great Central Railway in 1906/07. They were, in effect, three cylinder versions of existing 0-8-0 tender engines (later LNER Q4 class), and were developed specifically for shunting at the new hump yard at Wath-on-Dearne. In 1932 Nigel Gresley fitted one of the engines with a booster – this was a form of 'auxiliary' engine which provided extra power, via a pair of 10in x 12in cylinders, through the front axle of the bogie. Gresley had, in fact, ordered three boosters, but rather than fit the other two to existing S1s, it was considered more cost effective to build completely new engines and to incorporate the boosters in those from the outset. The two

The last N15X 4-6-0 to survive was No.32331 BEATTIE. It is believed that its final revenue earning duty was a ramblers' special from London Bridge to Windsor & Eton Riverside on 23 June 1957, which is seen leaving Knights Hill Tunnel near Tulse Hill. PHOTOGRAPH: R.C.RILEY

You'll Remember those Black and White Days...

The last two S1 0-8-4Ts – Nos.69901 and 69905 – were withdrawn from Frodingham shed in January 1957. Although many heavy shunting locomotives were rendered redundant by the ubiquitous 350hp diesel shunters, the S1s were displaced from their regular duties at Frodingham by another steam class – the J50 0-6-0Ts. This picture shows No.69905 a couple of years earlier at Doncaster shed, where its principal duty had been shunting rows of dead engines. PHOTOGRAPH: BRIAN MORRISON

brand-new booster-fitted S1s were built at Gorton Works in 1932 and were allocated to Mexborough shed for duties at Wath; this enabled two non-booster examples to be transferred to March for use at Whitemoor Yard.

Under BR auspices the S1s became Nos.69900-69905. By this time, the three booster-fitted locomotives had reverted to conventional format, their boosters having been removed in 1943. In 1949 the two S1s at Whitemoor were displaced by diesel shunters; they were transferred to Frodingham, but in 1950 they moved on to Mexborough where they joined their other classmates. In 1953 the S1s' duties at Wath were taken over by diesel shunters, and attempts were subsequently made to find something useful for the S1s to do; these attempts included trials at Immingham (as docks pilot) and at Doncaster (as shed pilot), but the engines were not altogether successful at the former, and were totally wasted at the latter. Nevertheless, Nos.69901 and 69905 were eventually found alternative work at Frodingham (again!), and while their four classmates were withdrawn – one in 1954 and three in 1956 – the pair at Frodingham survived until January 1957.

GCR 5A (LNER J63) 0-6-0T
To replace obsolete engine types on dock shunting duties, in 1906 the GCR introduced six small 0-6-0Ts with 3ft 6in wheels; they were, in effect, side tank versions of an earlier Pollitt saddle tank design. A seventh 0-6-0T was added in 1914.

Under LNER auspices the dock shunters were classified J63, and in BR days the class became Nos.68204-68210. At the start of the 1950s all seven were at Immingham. One of the class was withdrawn in 1953, two in 1955 and three in 1956, leaving No.68210 as the sole survivor. It did not have too long to bask in its glory as, like its classmates, it was soon displaced by new diesel shunters. It was withdrawn in February 1957.

LNER V4 2-6-2s
Without wishing to further the age-old 'Edward Thompson versus Nigel Gresley' debate, it could be argued that Gresley's V4 2-6-2s were the epitome of everything Thompson disliked - they were expensive to build and maintain, very much non-standard and, sin of sins, when Thompson took office the V4 class comprised only two engines. The criticisms regarding costs were perhaps justified, as the V4s incorporated a number of innovative (i.e. costly) features in order to minimise their axleweights. The emphasis on a light axleweight was because the engines were intended for widespread use on secondary and

branch duties, and this prompted familiar cries of 'Rolls Royces doing Ford jobs'. (Where have we heard that before?). Such extravagance – real or imagined – was anathema to Edward Thompson.

The two V4s were completed at Doncaster Works early in 1941, only a matter of weeks before Sir Nigel Gresley's death on 5 April. They were Gresley's very last new design. The V4s quickly proved to be very efficient and powerful engines, but they found no favour with Edward Thompson who addressed the shortage of 'secondary' engines by introducing, instead, the somewhat basic B1 4-6-0s. And so the V4 class remained just two in number. Under BR auspices they became Nos.61700 and 61701. The former was named BANTAM COCK, but although the latter was officially unnamed, it was invariably referred to as 'Bantam Hen'.

At the start of the BR era the two locomotives were allocated to Eastfield shed, from where they were their principal duties were on the West Highland line. This was followed by a period on general goods workings, principally to Dundee and Edinburgh. In May 1954 both V4s were transferred to Aberdeen (Ferryhill), from where they undertook goods workings principally to Dundee and Edinburgh, although in 1954/55 they had a period on secondment to the GNS Section. As

The D20 4-4-0s were extremely elegant engines, though by the mid-1950s the survivors were often poorly maintained. The last seven were withdrawn in 1957. One of the earlier withdrawals was No.62374, which posed for this superbly atmospheric picture at Selby shed. PHOTOGRAPH: BRIAN MORRISON

a numerically small and non-standard class, it was virtually inevitable that the V4s would not enjoy a lengthy life. For No.61700, withdrawal came in March 1957, and for No.61700 in November. The latter engine remained at Ferryhill shed until 23 January 1958, when it finally departed for Kilmarnock to be cut up.

With the benefit of hindsight, one might query why neither engine was saved for preservation. After all, they represented the very last new design from one of Britain's most famous and innovative locomotive engineers. It was a significant loss. Alternatively, one might speculate how British steam locomotive design and development might have differed if Nigel Gresley had lived a few years longer. Perhaps the V4s would have been built in considerable numbers to fill their anticipated role as the LNER's standard branch and secondary engines, and perhaps the existence of a substantial number of the lightweight, powerful, efficient (and fairly new) V4s, with their wide route availability, would have influenced the post-Nationalisation thinking about standard designs. Gresley-designed V4s instead of Standard 2-6-0s and 4-6-0s? The 1950s could have been very different...

Furness Railway 3F 0-6-0s
Six Furness Railway 0-6-0s survived long enough to be taken into BR stock. That was, in itself, quite noteworthy as the LMSR had dispensed with a huge number of pre-grouping locomotives (especially non-Midland types!) during its standardisation programme of the 1930s, and many classes had been rendered extinct. The

six Furness engines in question – along with four others which did not survive until the BR era – had been fitted with L&Y-type Class O Belpaire boilers during the LMS era (although one of the six – No.12494 reverted to a non-Belpaire boiler). Of the six Furness stalwarts, the last three examples clung on until 1957; they were No.52499, which was withdrawn from Workington shed in February, No.52501, which went from Carnforth in June, and No.52510, retired from Carnforth in August. That last survivor had been built by the North British Locomotive Company in 1920 as Furness No.33, and in common with most other FR engines it remained almost exclusively on its native territory. Its usual duties were unglamorous freight workings in Westmorland and Cumberland, but it nevertheless managed to notch up a very respectable 633,948 miles during its 37-year life.

LSWR C14 0-4-0Ts
Although the only two C14s in running stock were withdrawn in 1957, another representative remained in departmental stock for a little longer. However, for the sake of completeness, a brief word is in order here. The C14s started life as 2-2-0s and were introduced specifically for working light motor trains – they were, to all intents and purposes, intended to be 'detachable' power units for railmotors. They were, however, underpowered, and of the ten which were built, six were sold to private users and the other four were converted to 0-4-0Ts for light shunting duties. One of the 0-4-0T conversions was later sold, leaving three to be taken into BR stock

in 1948. Two of these were in running stock (Nos.30588 and 30589), while the third (No.77S) was in departmental stock.

Nos.30588 and 30589 were used at Southampton Town Quay. The latter was withdrawn in June 1957, leaving the former to soldier on alone until the end of the year when it, too, was retired. The replacement was 0-6-0 diesel No.11223, but that encountered problems on the sharper curves at the docks and so the departmental C14, No.77S, had to be requisitioned from Redbridge sleeper works.

GER (LNER Y4) 0-4-0Ts
As with the ex-LSWR C14 'motor tanks', the last ex-GER Y4 0-4-0T in running stock was withdrawn in 1957 but an example lingered on in departmental stock for a few years longer. The Y4 class – BR Nos.68125-68129 – comprised five short-wheelbase shunting engines which had been built to an Alfred Hill design - one in 1913, two in 1914 and two in 1921. The last survivor in running stock was No.68126, withdrawn from Stratford in October 1957 after being displaced by a four-wheeled diesel shunter; latterly its principal duties had been at Mile End (Devonshire Street) and Canning Town goods yard. Despite the withdrawal of No.68126, the Y4 flag was still flown by Departmental No.33 (formerly BR No.68129), which remained active on shunting duties at Stratford Old Works until 1963.

Back from the dead
Although various historic locomotives – or representatives of historic types – had been preserved prior to 1957, in those days the idea of returning a preserved locomotive to traffic was very novel. This was, after all, a time when working steam locomotives were two a penny, and several of those in everyday service had some sort of claim to fame. The bottom line was that preservationists could afford to be very choosy. This was clearly evidenced by a proposal made in 1957 to preserve ex-Highland Railway 4-4-0 No.54398 BEN ALDER (which was in store at Boat of Garten); the proposal prompted the comment that '...there seems little purpose in preserving the locomotive as so little of the original remains'. Less than ten years later, enthusiasts were desperately trying to preserve almost anything with a chimney, whether it was original or not. Further evidence of the embarrassment of locomotive riches in 1957 was provided by the LNER V4 2-6-2s – Sir Nigel Gresley's very last new design; as noted earlier, the withdrawal of the two V4s brought no real protests, let alone offers of new homes. In 1957 there was, of course, also an element of 'it couldn't really happen' when it came to the extinction of steam

traction; at the start of the year there were some 17,000 steam locomotives in BR stock, and new ones were still being constructed.

Consequently, in 1957 the return to active service of a locomotive which had been a static museum exhibit for twenty-six years was viewed in some quarters as something of an eccentricity. The locomotive in question was GWR 4-4-0 CITY OF TRURO. Its niche in British railway history had been secured by its alleged achievement, in 1904, of the first 100mph-plus in Britain, although in later years considerable doubt was cast as to whether the locomotive had actually reached 100mph.

Early in January 1957, No.3717, as it then was, was towed from York to Swindon (part of its journey south being via the Great Central main line) where it was to be restored to full working order, principally for use on ceremonial workings or enthusiasts' specials. The engine – ostensibly on permanent loan to the Western Region – arrived at Swindon on 11 January. It was reboilered (boiler DG6025 in place of DC3181), was repainted in the 1903 style with the 'GWR' monogram on its tender, and reverted to its original number, 3440. It nevertheless retained the top feed and copper capped chimney, and was fitted with ATC, none of which it had had when new.

Following its restoration, CITY OF TRURO undertook its first running-in turns during the week ending 23 March; these were with the 11.55am Swindon-Didcot stopper and return. On 25 March it did two return trips between Swindon and Bristol. The engine's first chartered working was on 30 March, when it worked the Wolverhampton-Ruabon leg of the Paddington-Portmadoc 'Festiniog Railway Special'. Other special workings followed, including a Pontypridd-Swindon return trip on 23 April, and Swindon-Kingswear and return on 19 May. The latter trip was with an eight coach train, and CITY OF TRURO managed to maintain a speed of around 60mph for comparatively lengthy stretches at a time. Unfortunately, though, on the return trip it developed big end trouble and had to be taken off at Chippenham.

Between its various special duties, CITY OF TRURO had regular outings on scheduled services, most usually on the 12.42pm Didcot-Southampton Terminus and returning with the 4.56pm from Southampton. On 16 June the engine was booked for an eight-coach SLS special from Wolverhampton-Swindon and return, and on the homeward trip speeds of 80mph were logged on the Swindon-Didcot and Banbury-Leamington sections. Less auspicious was the working of a Llanelly-Swindon special on 2 July - prior to the outward trip CITY OF TRURO suffered damage to its safety valves while coaling at Llanelly and had to be taken out of service. The necessary repairs were subsequently undertaken at Caerphilly Works. In order to prevent a recurrence of the accident, later in 1957 it was fitted with a shorter safety valve bonnet. Of the various specials which CITY OF TRURO worked during 1957, perhaps one other deserves a mention. This was a Plymouth-Penzance excursion on 15 September, which was believed to be the very first time a City had ever visited Penzance. CITY OF TRURO continued to appear on special workings in subsequent years, but it was taken out of service again in May 1961 to become a static exhibit at the new museum at Swindon. It was, however, resuscitated again in September 1985.

In August 1957, the last ex-Furness Railway 0-6-0, No.52510, was retired from Carnforth shed. It is seen remarshalling the Egremont milk train at Moor Row. PHOTOGRAPH: F.W.SHUTTLEWORTH

You'll Remember those Black and White Days...

The new and the old

The following lists of locomotives built and withdrawn during 1957 have been collated from various sources, principal among them being the *Railway Observer* magazine, arguably the most reliable source of its kind.

NEW LOCOMOTIVES - 1957 (first sheds shown in brackets - for shed codes, see p.23-25)

Brighton Works:
BR Class 4 2-6-4T: 80151 (75A); 80152 (75A); 80153 (75A); 80154 (75A).
Total: 4

Derby Works:
BR Class 5 4-6-0: 73145 (65B); 73146 (65B); 73147 (65B); 73148 (65B); 73149 (65B); 73150 (65B); 73151 (65B); 73152 (65B); 73153 (65B); 73154 (65B).
Total: 9
350hp 0-6-0 diesel: 13125 (18A); 13126 (18A); 13295 (55B); 13296 (55B); 13297 (55B); 13337 (62A); 13338 (62A); 13339 (62A); 13340 (62A); 13341 (62A); 13342

(62C); 13343 (62C); 13344 (62C); 13345 (62C); 13346 (62C); 13347 (62B); 13348 (66B); 13349 (66B); 13350 (66B); 13351 (66B); 13352 (87F); 13353 (87F); 13354 (87F); 13355 (87F); 13356 (87F); 13357 (87F); D3358 (87F); D3359 (87F); D3360 (87F); D3361 (87F); 13362 (82C); 13363 (88B); 13364 (88B); 13365 (88B); 13366 (88B); D3367 (10A); D3368 (10A); D3369 (10A); D3370 (10A); D3371 (10A); D3372 (26A); D3373 (26A); D3374 (26A); D3375 (55D); D3376 (55D); D3377 (55D); D3378 (55D); D3379 (55D); D3380 (55D); D3381 (55E); D3382 (66B); D3383 (66B); D3384 (66B); D3385 (66B); D3386 (65A); D3387 (65A); D3388 (65A); D3389 (65A); D3390 (65A); D3391 (65A); D3392 (65A); D3393 (65A); D3394 (65A); D3395 (65A); D3396 (65A); D3397 (88B); D3398 (88B); D3399 (88B); D3400 (88B); D3401 (88B); D3402 (88B); D3403 (88B); D3404(88B); D3405 (88B); D3406 (88B); D3407 (88B);

D3422 (88B). *Total: 77*
Horwich Works:
BR Class 4 2-6-0: 76079 (10D); 76080 (24D); 76081 (24D); 76082 (24D); 76083 (24D); 76084(24D); 76085 (15C); 76086 (15C); 76087 (17F); 76088 (17F); 76089 (17F); 76090 (67A); 76091 (67A); 76092 (67A); 76093 (67A); 76094 (67A); 76095 (67A); 76096 (67A); 76097 (67A); 76098(67A); 76099 (67A). *Total: 21*
Doncaster Works:
BR Class 5 4-6-0: 73159 (34E); 73160 (52C); 73161 (52C); 73162 (50A); 73163 (50A); 73164 (50A); 73165 (50A); 73166 (50A); 73167 (50A); 73168 (50A); 73169 (50A); 73170 (50A); 73171(50A).
Total: 13
BR Class 4 2-6-0: 76100 (65D); 76101 (65D); 76102 (65D); 76103 (65D); 76104 (61A); 76105(61A); 76106 (61A); 76107 (61A); 76108 (61A); 76109 (62A); 76110 (62A); 76111 (62A); 76112 (68B); 76113 (65B); 76114 (65B). *Total: 15*
350hp 0-6-0 diesel: D3497 (30A); D3498 (30A); D3499 (30A). *Total: 3*

The new and the old at Devons Road on 31 August 1957. Immaculate new Bo-Bo (later Class 20) diesel-electric D8803 shows up in stark contrast to two grubby 3F 'Jinties' Nos.47483 and 47560. PHOTOGRAPH: BRIAN MORRISON

(35A); 92142 (35A); 92143 (35A); 92144 (35A); 92145 (35A); 92146 (35A); 92147 (35A); 92148 (35A); 92149 (35A); 92150 (18B); 92151 (21A); 92152 (21A); 92153 (18A); 92154 (15A); 92155 (21A); 92156 (18A); 92157 (18A); 92158 (18A); 92159 (15A); 92160 (15A); 92161 (18B); 92162 (18B); 92168 (36A); 92169 (36A); 92170 (36A). *Total: 47*
350hp 0-6-0 diesel: D3419 (88B); D3420 (88B); D3421 (88B). *Total: 3*

Hunslet Engine Co:
200hp 0-6-0 diesel: 11163 (32A); 11164 (41A); 11165 (41A); 11166 (32A); 11167 (32A); 11168 (32A); 11169 (32A); 11170 (32A); 11171 (32A); 11172 (32A); 11173 (32A); 11174 (32A); 11175 (32A). *Total: 13*

Andrew Barclay:
200hp 0-6-0 diesel: 11184 (40A); 11185 (40A); 11186 (40A). *Total: 3*

Drewry/R.S.H:
200hp 0-6-0 diesel: 11218 (52E); 11219 (52E); 11220 (73A); 11221 (73C); 11222 (75A); 11223 (73C); 11224 (73C); 11225 (73C); 11226 (73C); 11227 (72D); 11228 (72D); 11229 (72D); D2260 (56G); D2261 (56G); D2262 (55D); D2263 (55D); D2264 (56G); D2265 (56G). *Total: 18*

North British Loco Co:
200hp 0-4-0 diesel: 11708 (62B); 11709 (62B); 11710 (62B); 11711 (62B); 11712 (62B); 11713 (62B); 11714 (62B); 11715 (62B); 11716 (62B); 11717 (62B); 11718 (62C); 11719 (64A). *Total: 12*

Ruston & Hornsby:
88hp diesel: WR departmental No.20 (Reading signal stores) *Total: 1*

Brush Electric:
'Type 2' A1A-A1A diesel: D5500 (30A); D5501 (30A); D5502 (30A). *Total: 3*

Vulcan/English Electric:
'Type 1' Bo-Bo diesel: D8000 (1D); D8001 (1D); D8002 (1D); D8003 (1D); D8004 (1D); D8005 (1D); D8006 (1D); D8007 (1D); D8008 (1D); D8009 (1D); D8010 (1D); D8011 (1D); D8012 (1D); D8013 (1D); D8014 (1D); D8015 (1D). *Total: 16*

British Thompson Houston:
'Type 1' Bo-Bo diesel: D8200 (1D). *Total: 1*

Purchased from Ministry of Supply:
8F 2-8-0: 48773 (66A); 48774 (66A); 48775 (66A). *Total: 3*

Returned to traffic:
GWR City 4-4-0: 3440 CITY OF TRURO (82A) *Total: 1*

LOCOMOTIVES WITHDRAWN - 1957
Last sheds shown in brackets; italics denotes last of class
RR 'R' 0-6-2T: *36 (88B); 38 (88B)*; 42 (88B); 43 (88B) *Total: 4*
TVR 'A' 0-6-2T: 304 (88E); 305 (88A); 349 (88E); 361 (88A); 364 (88A); 370 (88E); *373 (88E);* 376 (88A); 381 (88E); 383 (88E); 385 (88A); *390 (88E);* 393 (88E); 397 (88E); 398 (88E) *Total: 15*
14XX 0-4-2T: 1400 (82C); 1403 (82F); 1414 (84F); 1415 (81C); 1422 (82C);

Darlington Works:
BR Class 2 2-6-2T: 84020 (74A); 84021 (74A); 84022 (74A); 84023 (74A); 84024 (74B); 84025 (74B); 84026 (74B); 84027 (74B); 84028 (74B); 84029 (74B). *Total: 10*
350hp 0-6-0 diesel: 13332 (41A); 13333 (41A); 13334 (41A); 13335 (41A); 13336 (41A); D3439 (34A); D3440 (34A); D3441 (34A); D3442 (34A); D3443 (34A); D3444 (34A); D3445 (35A); D3446 (35A); D3447 (35A); D3548 (35A); D3549 (35A); D3550 (35A); D3551 (35A); D3552 (35A); D3553 (35A); D3454 (56G); D3455 (56G); D3456 (56G); D3457 (55B); D3458 (55D); D3459 (73C); D3460 (73C); D3461 (73C); D3462 (73C); D3463 (73C); D3464 (73C); D3465 (73C); D3466 (73C); D3467 (73C); D3468 (73C); D3469 (73C); D3470 (73C); D3471 (73C); D3472 (73C); D3473 (35A); D3474 (35A); D3475 (35A); D3476 (34A); D3477 (34A). *Total: 44*

Swindon Works:
BR Class 4 4-6-0: 75053 (6A); 75054 (6A); 75055 (15D); 75056 (16A); 75057 (15C); 75058 (15C); 75059 (15C); 75059 (15C); 75060 (15C); 75061 (15C); 75062 (16A); 75063 (16A); 75064 (16A). *Total: 12*
BR 9F 2-10-0: 92093 (36A); 92094 (36A); 92095 (38B); 92096 (38B); 92178 (35A); 92179 (35A); 92180 (35A); 92181 (35A); 92182 (35A); 92183 (35A). *Total: 10*
204hp 0-6-0 diesel: D2000 (34A); D2001 (34A); D2002 (34A); D2003 (34A). *Total: 4*

Crewe Works:
BR 9F 2-10-0: 92119 (18B); 92120 (18B); 92121 (15A); 92122 (15A); 92123 (15A); 92124 (15A); 92125 (15A); 92126 (15A); 92127 (15A); 92128 (18A); 92129 (21A); 92130 (21A); 92131 (21A); 92132 (21A); 92133 (21A); 92134 (21A); 92135 (21A); 92136 (21A); 92137 (21A); 92138 (21A); 92139 (21A); 92140 (35A); 92141

The Brush Electric Type 2 (later Class 31) diesels made their debut in 1957. The class eventually comprised 200 locomotives, but delivery was a protracted affair, the last not entering service until April 1961. One of the many later ones, D5531, stands in Doncaster Works yard awaiting commissioning. PHOTOGRAPH: BRIAN MORRISON

1439 (83A); 1443 (81C) *Total: 7*
2021 0-6-0PT: 2027 (87F); 2134 (6C); 2160 (6C) *Total: 3*
Dean Goods 0-6-0: *2538 (89A) Total: 1*
ROD 2-8-0: 3018 (82C) *Total: 1*
31XX 2-6-2T: 3100 (86F); 3101 (84E); 3104 (84A) *Total: 3*
3150 2-6-2T: 3150 (86E); 3163 (85B); 3171 (85B); 3172 (86E); 3176 (86E); 3177 (86E); 3180 (85B); 3183 (86E); 3186 (83D); 3187 (83D) *Total: 10*
Castle 4-6-0: 4000 NORTH STAR (87E) *Total: 1*

Star 4-6-0: *4056 PRINCESS MARGARET (82A)*; 4061 GLASTONBURY ABBEY (84A) *Total: 2*
43XX 2-6-0: 4326 (84F); 5314 (82F); 5325 (84E); 5334 (86C); 5391 (84E) *Total: 5*
45XX 2-6-2T: 4505 (83G); 4538 (82C); 4548 (83C); 4596 (85A); 5505 (83F); 5512 (82A); 5513 (87H); 5535 (82A) *Total: 8*
51XX 2-6-2T: 5107 (84F); 5109 (84F); 5161 (84D) *Total: 3*
54XX 0-6-0PT: 5401 (89A); 5403 (82D);

5404 (84C); 5405 (89A); 5406 (82D); 5413 (85B); 5415 (81C) *Total: 7*
57XX 0-6-0PT: 5710 (88A); 5712 (84H); 5723 (84K); 5724 (88A); 5729 (86H); 5735 (81E); 5741 (86B); 5760 (83B); 6708 (88B); 6710 (86B); 6713 (87K); 6730 (86B); 6737 (82C); 7792 (82C); 8755 (81A) *Total: 15*
58XX 0-4-2T: 5803 (89C); 5806 (89A); 5807 (85C); 5808 (81F); 5811 (81F); 5812 (89A); 5813 (84D); 5814 (85C); 5816 (81F); 5817 (85A); 5819 (87G) *Total: 11*
81XX 2-6-2T: 8105 (85A) *Total: 1*
90XX 4-4-0: 9008 (89C); 9009 (89C); 9010 (89C); 9011 (82C); 9012 (89C); 9016 (89C); 9020 (89C); 9022 (89C); 9023 (82C); 9024 (89C); 9025 (89C); 9026 (89A); 9027 (89A); 9028 (84J) *Total: 14*
LSWR M7 0-4-4T: 30041 (70B); 30042 (70B); 30244 (70A); 30250 (72E) *Total: 4*
LSWR B4 0-4-0T: 30082 (71A); 30094 (72D) *Total: 2*
LSWR O2 0-4-4T: 30207 (70F); 30216 (72D) *Total: 2*
LSWR T9 4-4-0: 30283 (71A); 30304 (72B); 30730 (70F) *Total: 3*
LSWR H15 4-6-0: 30330 (72B); 30483 (70A); 30487 (70A) *Total: 3*
LSWR 0395 0-6-0: 30572 (70B); 30574 (70C); 30578 (70C); 30580 (70C) *Total: 4*
LSWR C14 0-4-0T: 30588 (71A); 30589 (71A) *Total: 2*
LSWR 700 0-6-0: 30688 (70B) *Total: 1*
LSWR King Arthur 4-6-0: 30739 KING LEODEGRANCE (71B); 30742 CAMELOT (71B); 30748 VIVIEN

Fourteen of the twenty-nine ex-GWR 90XX class 4-4-0s were withdrawn during 1957. One of those to go was No.9012 which, although being officially allocated to Machynlleth shed at the time of withdrawal in July 1957, had been in store at Swindon since the previous year. On Saturday 16 June 1956 – its last Summer of revenue-earning activity – No.9012 is seen leaving Llanymynech station bound, presumably with the early evening train to Welshpool. The lines on the extreme left, incidentally, are those of the old Shropshire & Montgomeryshire Light Railway. PHOTOGRAPH: ALAN JARVIS

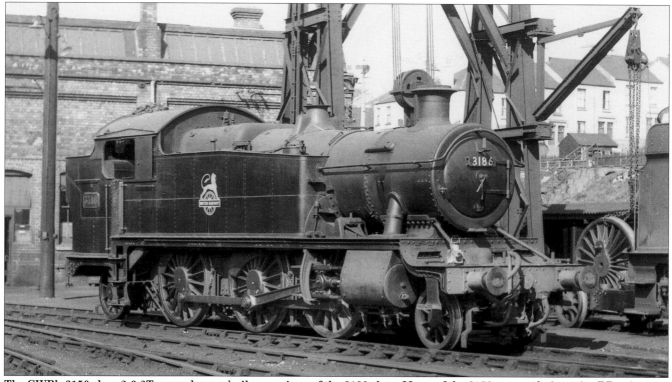

The GWR's 3150 class 2-6-2Ts were larger-boiler versions of the 3100 class. Many of the 3150s spent their entire BR existence based at Severn Tunnel Junction for banking duties through the Severn Tunnel, but one which enjoyed the less sulphurous atmosphere of South Devon was No.3186, which for several years was based at Laira. No.3186 was one of ten 3150s to be withdrawn in 1957; this left just only three of the class in service, and all three were withdrawn in 1958.

(70D); 30749 ISEULT (70D); 30750 MORGAN LE FAY (70D); 30751 ETARRE (70D); 30753 MELISANDE (70D); 30755 THE RED KNIGHT (70D) *Total: 8*

PDSWJ 0-6-2T: *30757 EARL OF MOUNT EDGCUMBE (71A) Total: 1*

SECR H 0-4-4T: 31274 (74E); 31321 (73A) *Total: 2*

SECR C 0-6-0: 31508 (73D); 31711 (73D); 31712 (73D) *Total: 3*

SECR P 0-6-0T: 31557 (73A) *Total: 1*

LBSC E3 0-6-2T: 32170 (73B); 32458 (73B); 32461 (73B); 32462 (73B) *Total: 4*

LBSC/SR Remembrance 4-6-0: *32331 BEATTIE (70D) Total: 1*

LBSC E6/E6X 0-6-2T: 32407 (75C); 32412 (73B) *Total: 2*

LBSC C2X 0-6-0: 32434 (75A); 32537 (73B) *Total: 2*

LBSC E4 0-6-2T: 32476 (70A); 32485 (75A); 32488 (74D); 32492 (70A); 32499 (70A); 32520 (75E) *Total: 6*

LBSC/SR E1R 0-6-2T: 32608 (72F); 32695 (72A) *Total: 2*

LBSC E1 0-6-0T: W1 MEDINA (70G) *Total: 1*

MR 2P 4-4-0: 40356 (17B); 40404 (17A); 40409 (24G); 40414 (17B); 40418 (17A); 40426 (22A); 40433 (14B); 40450 (10C); 40458 (16A); 40482 (19B); 40485 (15C); 40486 (22A); 40495 (21B); 40509 (71G); 40519 (17B); 40520 (55D); 40525 (17B); 40559 (6A); 40676 (10C) *Total: 19*

LMS 4P 4-4-0: 40904 (64D); 40926 (5A); 40927 (17A); 40930 (22B); 40934 (22B); 41045 (24J); 41048 (19B); 41064 (21B); 41073 (21B); 41075 (55F); 41077 (17D); 41085 (27A); 41089 (21B); 41098

(24J); 41103 (17A); 41108 (11E); 41112 (24J); 41140 (21A); 41151 (11E); 41153 (21B); 41155 (68C); 41172 (2A); 41179 (68B); 41180 (21A); 41181 (22B); 41185 (17A); 41192 (17A); 41195 (22B); 41197 (24J) *Total: 30*

MR 0F 0-4-0T: 41530 (22B); 41534 (17A) *Total: 2*

MR 1F 0-6-0T: 41699 (17B); 41706 (18D); 41710 (17A); 41748 (22B); 41753 (6C); 41779 (36A); 41803 (18D); 41860 (87K) *Total: 8*

MR 3F 0-6-0: 43181 (19A); 43201 (71J); 43224 (18D); 43239 (16C); 43259 (17A); 43290 (17D); 43341 (19A); 43396 (6K); 43401 (16A); 43402 (17A); 43443 (21A); 43463 (19C); 43469 (17B); 43476 (55D); 43595 (19A); 43596 (16B); 43684 (21A); 43690 (21A); 43717 (9A); 43776 (17D); 43786 (2B); 43795 (18A); 43806 (15C) *Total: 23*

MR 4F 0-6-0: 43837 (21B); 43847 (17A); 43851 (55B); 43852 (55E); 43857 (19C); 43889 (18D); 43891 (18C); 43898 (15D); 43912 (21A); 43927 (39A); 43959 (18A); 43980 (11D); 43992 (20F); 43993 (18D); 44017 (17A); 44024 (5F); *Total: 16*

MR 3F 0-6-0T: 47206 (14A); 47227 (15C); 47240 (14A); 47243 (14B); 47258 (27B) *Total: 5*

LMS Beyer Garratt 2-6-6-2T: 47967 (18C); 47969 (18C); 47972 (18C); 47973 (18C); 47978 (18C); 47979 (18C); 47980 (18C); 47982 (18C); 47986 (18C); 47987 (18C); 47995 (18C) *Total: 11*

LNW 7F 0-8-0: 48907 (3C); 48914 (2A); 48917 (9D); 48940 (3B); 48944 (8C); 48952 (1E); 49005 (1E); 49024 (2C); 49033 (87K); 49035 (87K); 49046 (85C); 49051 (84G); 49057 (9D); 49066 (3C);

49068 (2B); 49088 (1A); 49108 (3C); 49148 (87K); 49161 (86K); 49167 (3B); 49172 (2B); 49189 (3D); 49202 (3A); 49214 (8C); 49223 (3A); 49230 (5B); 49239 (10D); 49247 (3B); 49254 (10C); 49271 (3C); 49316 (86K); 49318 (10D); 49341 (10A); 49367 (3A); 49385 (10A); 49390 (10B); 49393 (10A); 49536 (26E); 49538 (26C); 49545 (27B); 49547 (27B); 49555 (26B); 49560 (26A); 49566 (27B); 49657 (56E); 49659 (27B); 49664 (27B); 49672 (27B) *Total: 48*

L&Y 2P 2-4-2T: 50636 (55F); 50752 (56E); 50887 (26C) *Total: 3*

L&Y 0F 0-4-0T: 51212 (22A); 51234 (27A); 51240 (53E) *Total: 3*

L&Y 2F 0-6-0T: 51307 (26A); 51338 (26A); 51353 (8A); 51381 (26A); 51432 (53E); 51447 (26A); 51474 (24A); 51481 (26A); 51491 (10D); 51499 (26B); 51500 (26B); 51503 (53E); 51506 (24D) *Total: 13*

L&Y 3F 0-6-0: 52094 (26D); 52125 (10D); 52132 (26C); 52143 (10A); 52160 (27B); 52165 (26A); 52172 (6K); 52175 (8C); 52186 (56A); 52196 (10D); 52203 (24C); 52217 (56E); 52235 (56F); 52236 (56D); 52328 (26A); 52336 (56D); 52338 (10D); 52368 (24C); 52376 (56A); 52379 (27B); 52412 (27B); 52418 (12C); 52449 (10A); 52521 (56F); 52529 (24B); 52551 (10A); 52576 (56D) *Total: 28*

FR 3F 0-6-0: 52499 (12C); 52501 (11A); *52510 (11A) Total: 3*

CR 3P 4-4-0: 54440 (66D); 54441 (66D); 54452 (64C); 54453 (66D); 54456 (66D); 54458 (60A) *Total: 6*

HR 0P 0-4-4T: *55053 (60C) Total: 1*

CR 2P 0-4-4T: 55125 (68C); 55168 (66B) *Total: 2*

CR 0F 0-4-0ST: 56028 (66D) *Total: 1*

C14 0-4-0T No.30589 and B4 0-4-0T No.30082 were both withdrawn in 1957. They were photographed together at Eastleigh. PHOTOGRAPH: B.K.B.GREEN; INITIAL PHOTOGRAPHICS

CR 3F 0-6-0T: 56230 (65F); 56234 (68C); 56243 (68B); 56257 (67C); 56280 (66A); 56294 (66C); 56297 (65G); 56299 (60A); 56320 (66C); 56329 (67A); 56342 (66A); 56346 (66A); 56350 (67A); 56357 (66A); 56369 (67A) *Total: 15*

CR 2F 0-6-0: 57234 (67C); 57346 (65D); 57430 (66C); 57460 (63B) *Total: 4*

CR 3F 0-6-0: 57573 (67B); 57582 (66B) *Total: 2*

MR 1P 0-4-4T: 58083 (9D) *Total: 1*

MR 2F 0-6-0: 58114 (19C); 58121 (11B); 58136 (55B); 58140 (19A); 58142 (15C); 58156 (11B); 58187 (11B); 58188 (36A); 58189 (17D); 58206 (22B); 58216 (36A); 58288 (3D); 58299 (11B); 58306 (3E) *Total: 14*

NLR 2F 0-6-0T: 58856 (17D); 58859 (1D); 58860 (17D) *Total: 3*

GER/LNER B12/3 4-6-0: 61512 (30A); 61519 (32A); 61520 (32A); 61537 (32B); 61538 (35C); 61540 (32F); 61541 (35B); 61545 (32F); 61550 (30A); 61555 (31A); 61556 (32A); 61557 (30E); 61565 (35C); 61569 (32B); 61574 (35B); 61578 (30A); 61579 (30A) *Total: 17*

LNER V4 2-6-2: 61700 BANTAM COCK (61B); *61701 (61B) Total: 2*

GNR K2 2-6-0: 61726 (38A); 61729 (38A); 61730 (40B); 61732 (38A); 61733 (65C); 61735 (65C); 61736 (40B); 61744 (40F) *Total: 8*

GNSR D40 4-4-0: 62264 (61C) *Total: 1*

NER D20 4-4-0: 62375 (52D); 62381 (52D); 62383 (52D); 62387 (52D); 62395 (52D); 62396 (52D); 62397 (53D) *Total: 7*

NBR D30 4-4-0: 62419 MEG DODS (62A); 62420 DOMINIE SAMPSON (64G); 62423 DUGALD DALGETTY (64G); 62424 CLAVERHOUSE (64A); 62429 THE ABBOT (62A); 62430 JINGLING GEORDIE (62A); 62435 NORNA (64G); 62438 PETER POUNDTEXT (62B) *Total: 8*

GER/LNER D16/3 4-4-0: 62510 (31C); 62514 (31C); 62516 (31C); 62519 (32G); 62526 (31B); 62533 (32G); 62535 (40A); 65239 (31A); 62546 CLAUD HAMILTON (32D); 62548 (31B); 62553 (31A); 62556 (32A); 62558 (31C); 62562 (31B); 62565 (31C); 62575 (31C); 62576 (31A); 62578 (32G); 62584 (31C); 62593 (32A); 62596 (32A); 62601 (31C); 62605 (31B); 62608 (31A); 62609 (35C); 62611 (32D); 62617 (32G); 62619 (32A) *Total: 28*

LNER D49 and D49/1 4-4-0: 62713 ABERDEENSHIRE (62A); 62724 BEDFORDSHIRE (53B); 62726 THE MEYNELL (50E); 62748 THE SOUTHWOLD (50B); 62757 THE BURTON (53B); 62758 THE CATTISTOCK (50D); 62761 THE DERWENT (50C) *Total: 7*

GER E4 2-4-0: 62789 (31A); 62796 (31A) *Total: 2*

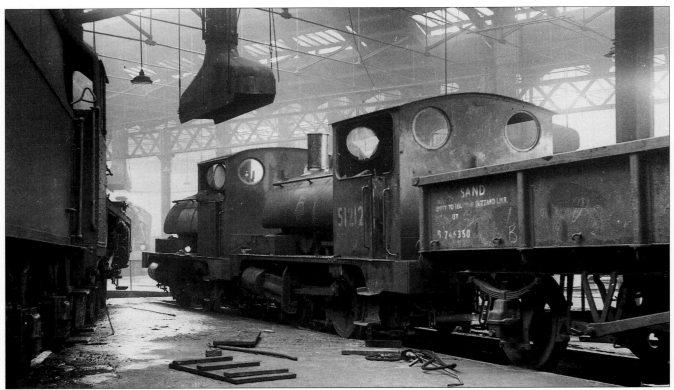

A lovely atmospheric shot of ex-L&Y Pugs Nos.51212 and 51202 at Barrow Road shed in Bristol. Following the withdrawal of No.51212 in 1957, another of the class, No.51217, was transferred to Barrow Road to take its place; since 1952 the Pugs had been used on the Avonside Wharf siding, where heavier locomotives were prohibited. The last two Lanky Pugs at Barrow Road were Nos.51217 and 51218, which were ousted by 204hp diesels in 1961. PHOTOGRAPH: IVO PETERS

You'll Remember those Black and White Days...

At the start of 1957 just three of the delightful E4 2-4-0s were left in service. All were based at Cambridge. Of the three, Nos.62789 and 62796 were withdrawn during 1957, leaving only No.62785 in service; somewhat remarkably, perhaps, that last representative soldiered on until December 1959. One of the two 1957 withdrawals – No.62789 – is seen approaching Trumpington signal box, on the main line just to the south of Cambridge, with the 1.34pm train to Marks Tey and Colchester. PHOTOGRAPH: J.A.COILEY

GNR J6 0-6-0: 64193 (36A); 64204 (40F) *Total: 2*
GCR J11 0-6-0: 64293 (40E); 64295 (36E); 64300 (38E); 64303 (40A); 64312 (40B); 64320 (40B); 64322 (39A); 64327 (38E); 64330 (38E); 64349 (39A); 64372 (40B); 64399 (36D); 64401 (39A); 64411 (40B); 64412 (41A); 64414 (40E); 64432 (36B); 64448 (36D); 64453 (38C) *Total: 19*
NER J21 0-6-0: 65078 (52D); 65091 (52D) *Total: 2*
GCR J10 0-6-0: 65159 (10A); 65186 (17F) *Total: 2*
NBR J36 0-6-0: 65213 (61A); 65225 (64F); 65242 (61A); 65244 (64E); 65250 (64F); 65324 (65C) *Total: 6*
GER J15 0-6-0: 65356 (31B) *Total: 1*
GER J17 0-6-0: 65523 (30A); 65537 (32A); 65572 (31B) *Total: 3*
NER J25 0-6-0: 65650 (50B); 65680 (54B) *Total: 2*
GER F5 2-4-2T: 67193 (30A); 67199 (30A); 67200 (30A); 67202 (30A); 67203 (30A); 67208 (30A); 67209 (30A) *Total: 7*

GER F6 2-4-2T: 67221 (30A) *Total: 1*
NER G5 0-4-4T: 67248 (50F); 67250 (50C); 67254 (54A); 67256 (53D); 67258 (54A); 67259 (54A); 67273 (50C); 67277 (52F); 67278 (54A); 67282 (53B); 67294 (54A); 67318 (54A); 67319 (50F); 67321 (54A); 67324 (51G); 67326 (52D); 67337 (51D); 67338 (54A); 67339 (52F); 67343 (54A); 67346 (50F) *Total: 21*
GNR C12 4-4-2T: 67395 (31A) *Total: 1*
GCR C13 4-4-2T: 67413 (6D); 67419 (39A); 67423 (36D); 67428 (6E); 67434 (36D); 67437 (39A) *Total: 6*
GCR C14 4-4-2T: 67440 (39A); 67441 (39A); 67442 (6E); 67443 (39A); 67444 (39A); 67446 (39A); 67449 (6E); 67451 (39A) *Total: 8*
NBR Y9 0-4-0ST: 68106 (65E); 68115 (64A) *Total: 2*
GER Y4 0-4-0T: 68126 (30A) *Total: 1*
Sentinel Y1 0-4-0T: 68142 (51E); 68145 (53D) *Total: 2*
Sentinel Y3 0-4-0T: 68159 (52A) *Total: 1*
GCR J63 0-6-0T: *68210 (40B)* *Total: 1*
NER J71 0-6-0T: 68232 (53A); 68252 (53A); 68253 (50A); 68266 (54B); 68267 (52A); 68273 (50A); 68279 (51A); 68280 (50A); 68298 (53A) *Total: 9*
NBR J88 0-6-0T: 68351 (62C) *Total: 1*
NER J73 0-6-0T: 68362 (50C) *Total: 1*
NER J77 0-6-0T: 68391 (51F); 68412 (51E); 68423 (51G); 68426 (52F); 68434 (50D) *Total: 5*
NBR J83 0-6-0T: 68450 (64A); 68465 (62B) *Total: 2*
GER J67/69 0-6-0T: 68503 (65C); 68515 (32G); 68516 (30A); 68512 (38D); 68551 (62B); 68567 (31A); 68595 (6E); 68598 (6E); 68610 (34D) *Total: 9*

'Claud Hamilton' 4-4-0 No.62617 was withdrawn from Melton Constable shed – the heart of the old Midland & Great Northern system – in May 1957. A few years earlier, it was seen on an East Dereham-Wymondham working.

GNR J52 0-6-0T: 68761 (36A); 68768 (38A); 68778 (36A); 68784 (36A); 68808 (34B); 68811 (36A); 68823 (36A); 68826 (38A); 68832 (34A); 68841 (36A); 68843 (36A); 68849 (36A); 68851 (38A); 68860 (38A); 68874 (34A); 68886 (36A); 68887 (38A); 68888 (34A) *Total: 18*

NER N10 0-6-2T: 69093 (54B); 69094 (53A); 69096 (53A); 69098 (50B); 69100 (52A); 69107 (53A); 69108 (53A) *Total: 7*

NBR N15 0-6-2T: 69130 (64A); 69167 (64A); 69210 (65C) *Total: 3*

MSL N5 0-6-2T: 69261 (40E); 69302 (41A); 69312 (41A); 69316 (41A); 69326 (17F); 69328 (39A); 69331 (17E); 69346 (6E); 69347 (17F); 69348 (41A); 69350 (34E); 69356 (27E); 69365 (36D); 69369 (40B) *Total: 14*

GNR N1 0-6-2T: 69440 (56B); 69457 (56C); 69469 (56C); 69484 (56B) *Total: 4*

LNER N2 0-6-2T: 69500 (65C); 69501 (34B); 69503 (61B); 69519 (34A); 69557 (34D); 69558 (34A); 69559 (34A); 69566 (34A); 69590 (34A); 69595 (65C) *Total: 10*

GER N7 0-6-2T: 69689 (32D) *Total: 1*

NER A7 4-6-2T: 69772 (53C); 69782 (53C); 69786 (53C) *Total: 3*

CR A5 4-6-2T: 69815 (39A); 69833 (51A) *Total: 2*

LNER A8 4-4-2T: 69868 (51F); 69876 (51D) *Total: 2*

GCR/LNER S1 0-8-4T: 69901 (36C); *69905 (36C) Total: 2*

NER T1 4-8-0T: 69911 (51B); 69913 (50A); 69916 (50A) *Total: 3*

The Great North of Scotland Railway did a fine line in 4-4-0s, two classes of which – D40 and D41 – were represented in BR days. Most of the remaining D40s were withdrawn during the mid-1950s, having been displaced on the old GNS Section by B12 4-6-0s, and following the retirement of No.62264 in February 1957 (seen here on an unidentified freight working) only No.62277 GORDON HIGHLANDER remained. Fortunately, though, No.62277 was saved for preservation, and reverted to its original guise of No.49. PHOTOGRAPH: PAUL CHANCELLOR COLLECTION

Following the introduction of DMUs in the Manchester area, withdrawal of the ex-Great Central C14 4-4-2Ts commenced in 1957. Eight of the twelve class members were retired before the year was out; the very first of the eight to go was No.67451, withdrawn from Gorton shed in January. It is seen at Marple on a Manchester-Hayfield working. PHOTOGRAPH: R.BAXTER